CLASSIC CARS

Lynda Springate

HarperCollins*Publishers*

HarperCollins Publishers
P.O. Box, Glasgow, G4 0NB

First published 1996

Reprint 10 9 8 7 6 5 4 3 2 1 0

© Text, HarperCollins Publishers, 1996
© Internal photographs, National Motor Museum, Beaulieu, 1996

Cover photograph: Bentley 4.5 Litre (© Susan Wakeford)

ISBN 0 00 470944-6

Printed in Italy by Amadeus S.p.A.

CONTENTS

CONTENTS

CONTENTS

CONTENTS

AC Cobra 427

AC Cobras were assembled in the USA with chassis and bodies supplied by AC of Great Britain, and were powered by a Ford V8 engine. The 427 Cobra was one of the highest-performance road/racing cars ever produced. It was capable of 0–100 mph/160 kph in 8.8 seconds. Also available was the 289 with a smaller 4747 cc engine.

Engine	8 cylinder 6997 cc 410 bhp
Length	13 ft/3.96 m
Width	5 ft 6 in/1.68 m
Top speed	165 mph/264 kph
Price new	$7495
Current	1965–66

Alfa Romeo 8C 2300

Alfa Romeo had an enviable reputation for producing fast and stylish racing and sports cars. Its racing team was managed by Enzo Ferrari until 1938. An 8C 2300 driven by Tazio Nuvolari won the Targa Florio in Italy in 1931. The cars then went on to win the Le Mans 24-hour race three years running. Standard road cars were fitted with a detuned racing unit that could provide a 0–50 mph/80 kph acceleration time of 7 seconds.

Engine	8 cylinder 2336 cc 165 bhp
Length	14 ft 9 in/4.50 m
Width	5 ft 6 in/1.68 m
Top speed	115 mph/184 kph
Price new	£3000
Current	1931–35

Alfa Romeo Montreal

Italian stylist Bertone produced an Alfa Romeo-based show car for the 1967 Expo at Montreal. The car went into production in 1970 as the Montreal. It was styled as a sports coupé but with a rear hatchback. Other features included front-wheel drive, electronic ignition and fuel injection. 0–60 mph/96 kph took 7.6 seconds.

Engine	8 cylinder 2593 cc 200 bhp
Length	13 ft 10 in/4.22 m
Width	5 ft 6 in/1.68 m
Top speed	137 mph/219 kph
Price new	£4999
Current	1970–77

Alfa Romeo 2000 GTV Spider

The distinctive shape of the 2000 dates back to Pininfarina's original 1966 design for the 1570 cc Duetto, which was the car used by Dustin Hoffman in the groundbreaking film *The Graduate*. Capable of 0–60 mph/96 kph in 9.7 seconds, the Alfa Romeo 2000 GTV had a five-speed gearbox and servo disc brakes. A totally new version of the Spider was introduced in 1995.

Engine	4 cylinder 1962 cc 132 bhp
Length	13 ft 5 in/4.09 m
Width	5 ft 2 in/1.57 m
Top speed	118 mph/189 kph
Price new	£2999
Current	1970–95

Alfa Romeo 1600 GT Junior

Based on the 1300 GT Junior, the 1600 had a five-speed gear-box and all-round disc brakes. Performance of the 1570 cc engine was helped by two Weber carburettors. It could cover a quarter of a mile/0.4 km from a standing start in 18 seconds. The 1300 and 1600 GT models were styled by Bertone, who produced the original design in 1966.

Engine	4 cylinder 1570 cc 107 bhp
Length	13 ft 5 in/4.09 m
Width	5 ft 2 in/1.57 m
Top speed	115 mph/184 kph
Price new	£2399
Current	1973–76

Alpine-Renault 1600S

Automobiles Alpine produced some of the most successful French sports cars. They were based on Renaults and the works cars were highly regarded as rally cars. The 1600S took the first three places in the Monte Carlo Rally of 1971. Engines were the same as those fitted to the Renault 16 and were all aluminium. 0–60 mph/96 kph in road-going trim took 6.3 seconds.

Engine	4 cylinder 1565 cc 125 bhp
Length	12 ft 11 in/3.94 m
Width	5 ft/1.52 m
Top speed	127 mph/203 kph
Price new	N/A
Current	1967–71

Alvis 12/40

Alvis introduced its 12/40 HP side-valve engine in 1922, and it soon gained the company a reputation for reliable touring cars. Such was their reliability that Alvis guaranteed that should one of its cars suffer any mechanical failure during its first year, Alvis would pay the owner £1 per day for the length of time it took to repair the car.

Engine	4 cylinder 1598 cc 38 bhp
Length	12 ft 10 in/3.91 m
Width	4 ft 11½ in/1.48 m
Top speed	60 mph/96 kph
Price new	£550
Current	1922–24

Alvis Speed 25

Following the success of its touring cars of the 1920s, Alvis developed larger versions for the 30s. One of the most highly regarded was the Speed 25 with a 3.5 litre engine. Sir Malcolm Campbell of *Bluebird* fame tested one and declared it to be a 'thoroughbred'. The Speed 25 had independent front suspension, an all-synchromesh gearbox and servo-assisted brakes. 0–60 mph/96 kph took 15 seconds.

Engine	6 cylinder 3571 cc 106 bhp
Length	15 ft 2½ in/4.64 m
Width	5 ft 6½ in/1.69 m
Top speed	95 mph/152 kph
Price new	£775 chassis only
Current	1935–39

Alvis TD 21

The Alvis TD 21 was a symbol of prestige in the 1960s. It was a comfortable touring car, with a well-built aluminium body. Although it was aimed at the more traditional car buyer, the pushrod OHV engine could power the car from a standing start to a quarter of a mile/0.4 km in 21 seconds. Top speed was in excess of 100 mph/160 kph. The TD 21 was styled by British coach-builder Park Ward, which adapted an earlier design by the Swiss company Graber.

Engine	6 cylinder 2993 cc 115 bhp
Length	15 ft 8 in/4.78 m
Width	5 ft 6 in/1.68 m
Top speed	103 mph/165 kph
Price new	£3012
Current	1959–63

Aston Martin DB5

The Aston Martin first appeared in the autumn of 1963 with three SU carburettors fitted as standard. A DB5 was the car driven by James Bond in the film *Goldfinger*. Performance was excellent, with 0–60 mph/96 kph reached in 7 seconds and a standing start to quarter of a mile/0.4 km in 15.4 seconds. An optional 'Vantage' engine could be fitted for £190. This boosted the bhp from 282 to 325.

Engine	6 cylinder 3995 cc 282 bhp
Length	15 ft/4.57 m
Width	5 ft 6 in/1.68 m
Top speed	145 mph/232 kph
Price new	£4175
Current	1963–65

Aston Martin Vantage Zagato

Aston Martin combined with the famous Italian coach-builder Zagato to produce a limited edition of 50 V8 Vantage Zagatos. The cars were aluminium bodied and 10% lighter than the V8 saloon. The aerodynamic shape was designed to give a Cd (drag coefficient) reading of 0.29. In addition to its top speed of 186 mph/298 kph, the Zagato could accelerate from 0–60 mph/96 kph in 4.8 seconds.

Engine	V8 5340 cc 432 bhp
Length	14 ft 4³/₄ in/4.39 m
Width	6 ft 1³/₄ in/1.87 m
Top speed	186 mph/298 kph
Price new	£87,000
Current	1986–90

Auburn 851 Speedster

Erret Lobban Cord, later to be well known for his connections with Cord and Duesenberg, bought the Auburn Motor Company in 1924. Auburn soon earned a reputation for luxury, style and performance. Each 851 Speedster had a dashboard-mounted plaque signed by Ab Jenkins, who personally tested them to the 100 mph limit.

Engine	8 cylinder 4585 cc 150 bhp
Length	16 ft 2½ in/4.94 m
Width	5 ft 11½ in/1.82 m
Top speed	100 mph/160 kph
Price new	£800
Current	1935–36

Audi Quattro

The Audi Quattro represented a great step forward in terms of car safety, as it was the first production car fitted with four-wheel drive as standard. It proved to be a highly successful rally car in the hands of drivers like Hannu Mikkola. Fitted with Bosch K-Jetronic injection and a KKK turbo-charger, the car could accelerate from 0–60 mph/96 kph in 6.5 seconds.

Engine	5 cylinder 2144 cc 200 bhp
Length	14 ft 5 in/4.39 m
Width	5 ft 7 in/1.70 m
Top speed	138 mph/221 kph
Price new	£14,500
Current	1980–present

Austin Seven

Herbert Austin produced the first Austin 7 HP in 1922. It was designed to be a full four-seater yet very cheap to buy. It was one of the first 'people's cars' and introduced less-wealthy families to motoring for the first time. By 1926 the Austin Seven had acquired an electric horn, speedometer, electric starter and shock absorbers.

Engine	4 cylinder 747 cc 10.5 bhp
Length	9 ft 2 in/2.79 m
Width	3 ft 10 in/1.17 m
Top speed	45 mph/72 kph
Price new	£135
Current	1922–38

Austin Seven Swallow

William Lyons, famous for his Jaguar cars, began manufacturing motorcycle sidecars in Blackpool under the name of Swallow in 1921. Later, his company made special bodywork on popular small car chassis, including Austins. One of his curvaceous styles on the Austin Seven saloon was designed especially to appeal to lady owner-drivers.

Engine	4 cylinder 747 cc 10.5 bhp
Length	9 ft 2 in/2.79 m
Width	3 ft 10 in/1.17 m
Top speed	50 mph/80 kph
Price new	£187
Current	1928–32

Austin A35

A more powerful version of the A30, Austin's little A35 was capable of nipping from 0–60 mph/96 kph in nearly half a minute and managed a standing start to quarter of a mile/0.4 km in 23.5 seconds. The A30/35 range was Austin's answer to the Issigonis-designed Morris Minor. It took part in saloon car racing with the OHV engine suitably tuned.

Engine	4 cylinder 948 cc 34 bhp
Length	11 ft 4^1/$_2$ in/3.47 m
Width	4 ft 7 in/1.40 m
Top speed	70 mph/112 kph
Price new	£569
Current	1956–62

Austin-Healey Frog-eye Sprite

So called because of its frog-eyed headlamps and smiling radiator grille, the Sprite was based mechanically on the Austin A35's front suspension with a Morris Minor steering rack. It was powered by the Austin 948 cc A series engine. Many Sprites took part in trials or were extensively tuned for rallying. A standard Frog-eye could do 0–50 mph/80 kph in 13.7 seconds.

Engine	4 cylinder 948 cc 50 bhp
Length	11 ft 5½ in/3.49 m
Width	4 ft 5 in/1.35 m
Top speed	82 mph/131 kph
Price new	£678
Current	1958–61

Austin-Healey 3000 Mk III

The Austin-Healey 3000 began life as the Healey 100 which was announced at the London Motor Show in 1952. The cars developed into the 100-6 and finally the 3000 in 1959. The 3000 Mk III was the most powerful and fastest of the series. Performance was helped by the addition of two 30 degree semi-downdraught carburettors. Its 0–60 mph/96 kph time was 9.8 seconds.

Engine	6 cylinder 2912 cc 148 bhp
Length	13 ft 1½ in/4 m
Width	5 ft/1.52 m
Top speed	121 mph/194 kph
Price new	£1106
Current	1959–67

Bentley 3 Litre

W.O. Bentley wanted to produce a fast sporting car that would be equally at home on open road or in town. He succeeded so well with the 3 litre Bentley that a number of different axle and wheelbase options were made available to suit all enthusiasts. Many of the open tourers had bodies fitted by the coach-builder Vanden Plas.

Engine	4 cylinder 2996 cc 15.9 HP
Length	13 ft 3 in/4.03 m
Width	5 ft 8 in/1.73 m
Top speed	85 mph/136 kph
Price new	£1125
Current	1920-29

Bentley 4.5 Litre

The successor to the 3 litre Bentley was the 4.5 litre, which appeared initially in unsupercharged form. Cars driven by 'The Bentley Boys' won the Le Mans 24-hour endurance race in 1924, 1927, 1928 and 1929. The supercharged version did not have such a spectacular racing career, but was generally agreed to be a fine road car.

Engine	4 cylinder 4398 cc 175 bhp
Length	14 ft 4½ in/4.38 m
Width	5 ft 8½ in/1.74 m
Top speed	120 mph/192 kph
Price new	£1750
Current	1927–31

Bentley R Type Continental

Introduced in 1952, the R Type Continental Bentley was for its time the fastest production saloon car in the world. It was fitted with twin SU carburettors, which helped it accelerate from 0–60 mph/96 kph in 10.8 seconds, and 0–100 mph/160 kph in 29.4 seconds. The car's elegant styling is admired by many. The bodywork is aluminium and most were built by coach-builders Mulliner and Park Ward.

Engine	6 cylinder 4556 cc
Length	17 ft 3 in/5.26 m
Width	5 ft 11 in/1.80 m
Top speed	115 mph/184 kph
Price new	£6928
Current	1952–55

Bentley Turbo R

Bentley began producing high-performance cars again with the Mulsanne Turbo of 1982. The Turbo R of 1985 was based on the Mulsanne but had much-improved roadholding, largely due to having stiffer suspension. Performance was also impressive. Fuelled by K Motronic injection, the V8 engine was capable of 0–60 mph/196 kph in 6.5 seconds.

Engine	V8 6750 cc 298 bhp
Length	17 ft 3 in/5.26 m
Width	6 ft 1 in/1.85 m
Top speed	134 mph/214 kph
Price new	£127,351
Current	1985–present

BMW 328

The BMW 328 was one of the most advanced sports cars of the 1930s. Its bodywork design was more like that of a post-war model in the way that it was styled; most noticeable were the faired-in headlamps and all-enclosed body. Frazer-Nash acquired the rights to produce BMWs in Britain. The cars had a top speed of nearly 100 mph/160 kph, and a 0–60 mph/96 kph time of 9.5 seconds.

Engine	6 cylinder 1971cc 100 bhp
Length	12 ft 10 in/3.91 m
Width	5 ft 3 in/1.60 m
Top speed	95 mph/152 kph
Price new	£695
Current	1936–39

BMW 507

One of the most striking of the early postwar BMWs was the two-seater 507. It was fitted with a new V8 engine developed by engineer Fritz Fiedler. It was the same engine as was originally fitted to the 502 model. The cars were fitted with twin downdraught Zenith carburettors. Only 252 BMW 507s were ever built. 0–60 mph/96 kph acceleration took 11.5 seconds.

Engine	V8 3168 cc 150 bhp
Length	14 ft 5 in/4.39 m
Width	5 ft 5 in/1.65 m
Top speed	118 mph/189 kph
Price new	£4201
Current	1955–59

BMW 3.0 CSL

The 3.0 CSL was BMW's fuel-injected version of its high-performance 3.0 CS series. All models were fitted with Bosch D Jetronic injection. Racing CSLs had extra spoilers in the form of aerodynamic wings. These wings caused the cars to be known as 'Batmobiles'. The smooth six-cylinder engine was able to accelerate from 0–60 mph/96 kph in 7.3 seconds. Standing start to quarter of a mile/0.4 km took 15.7 seconds.

Engine	6 cylinder 3003 cc 206 bhp
Length	15 ft 3 in/4.65 m
Width	5 ft 8$\frac{1}{2}$ in/1.74 m
Top speed	133 mph/213 kph
Price new	£7399
Current	1971–75

BMW M1

The BMW M1 was originally designed for homologation as a Pro-Car racer. A total of 457 were built, including the road-going cars. Italian car stylist Giugiaro was responsible for designing the bodywork. His design was of a mid-engined coupé made up of fibreglass panels. The M1 could accelerate from 0–30 mph/48 kph in 2.1 seconds, and 0–60 mph/96 kph took 5.5 seconds.

Engine	6 cylinder 3453 cc 277 bhp
Length	14 ft 3^1/$_2$ in/4.36 m
Width	6 ft/1.83 m
Top speed	162 mph/259 kph
Price new	£37,580
Current	1979–81

Borgward Isabella

The Borgward Isabella was designed by Carl Borgward of Bremen. Two versions were available: a roomy two-door saloon or a coupé. Borgwards were well built and could happily cruise at 80 mph/128 kph. They led many rival car manufacturers for several years until Borgward himself went bankrupt. The standard OHV engine could accelerate from 0–60 mph/96 kph in 17.6 seconds.

Engine	4 cylinder 1493 cc 82 bhp
Length	14 ft 5 in/4.39 m
Width	5 ft 7¼ in/1.71 m
Top speed	84 mph/134 kph
Price new	£1446
Current	1954–62

Bristol 404

The Bristol Aeroplane Company built its first car, the Type 400, which was based on the BMW 2 litre, in 1947. The company soon became well known as a builder of fast touring cars. The 404 of 1953 was known as 'The Businessman's Express'. A 140 bhp engine option was also available. A design feature was the non-opening boot lid.

Engine	6 cylinder 1971 cc 105 bhp
Length	14 ft 3$\frac{1}{4}$ in/4.35 m
Width	5 ft 8 in/1.73 m
Top speed	100 mph/160 kph
Price new	£3542
Current	1953–55

Bugatti Type 35

Bugatti introduced his Type 35 racing car in 1924. The aerodynamic shape was much admired for its elegance – even the flat-spoked aluminium wheels were carefully designed. A highly successful racing car, the Type 35 was unusual in that it was also offered for sale to the general public. Bugatti offered a supercharged version from 1925.

Engine	8 cylinder 1990 cc 110 bhp
Length	12 ft 1 in/3.68 m
Width	4 ft 9 in/1.45 m
Top speed	110 mph/176 kph
Price new	£1100
Current	1924–31

Bugatti Type 41

Ettore Bugatti only built six Type 41s, or Royales as they were otherwise known. They were intended to be the 'Cars of Kings' but no king ever bought one. Each car was bodied by a different coach-builder; the one illustrated was by Kellner of Paris. Royales had a straight-eight engine with overhead camshaft. These engines were also used in Bugatti railcars.

Engine	8 cylinder 12,760 cc 200 bhp
Length	15 ft 4 in/4.67 m
Width	5 ft 3 in/1.60 m
Top speed	80 mph/128 kph
Price new	£6500
Current	1927–33

Buick Skylark

The Skylark was Buick's version of a four-seater convertible sporting car for the 1950s. The car was based on the current Roadmaster chassis. It had independent front suspension and could manage 0–60 mph/96 kph in 12 seconds. Buick produced the Skylark in a limited edition run of 1690 in its Golden Anniversary year. The model name was revived in the 1960s.

Engine	V8 5230 cc 188 bhp
Length	17 ft 3½ in/5.27 m
Width	6 ft 8 in/2.03 m
Top speed	95 mph/152 kph
Price new	$5000
Current	1953

Cadillac Fleetwood Series 60

It was the fashion of American cars in the 1950s to be clothed in large amounts of chrome. The 1955 Cadillacs were no exception and wore huge chrome Dagmar bumpers at the front, and aircraft-like fins at the rear. Power steering was standard, as was air conditioning, self-tuning radio and automatic windscreen wash wipe. 0–60 mph/96 kph took 10 seconds.

Engine	V8 5420 cc 230 bhp
Length	18 ft 11½ in/5.77 m
Width	6 ft 8 in/2.03 m
Top speed	111 mph/178 kph
Price new	£3000
Current	1947–present

Cadillac Eldorado

Cadillac produced a convertible version of the legendary Eldorado series. It was known as the Biarritz and had a completely restyled body designed by Ron Hill. A hard-top version of the Biarritz was available at the same time and called the Seville. Although the two cars weighed over 4620 lb/2100 kg they could accelerate from 0–60 mph/96 kph in just over 12 seconds.

Engine	V8 5970 cc 325 bhp
Length	18 ft 6 in/5.64 m
Width	6 ft 8 in/2.03 m
Top speed	105 mph/168 kph
Price new	$7500
Current	1956–63

Chevrolet Corvette

Chevrolet's Corvette was one of the first mass-produced two-seater sports cars to be made in the USA. The body-work was made of fibreglass and it looked like a European sports car. It was quite small and had a minimum amount of chrome trim. The first Corvettes had a six-cylinder engine and two-speed powerglide gearbox. Acceleration from 0–60 mph/96 kph took 11 seconds.

Engine	6 cylinder 3861 cc 150 bhp
Length	13 ft 11 in/4.24 m
Width	6 ft/1.83 m
Top speed	106 mph/170 kph
Price new	$3523
Current	1953–present

Chevrolet Bel Air

The Chevrolet Bel Air was a popular American car. It had good performance and handling without being too expensive. Fuel injection was an option on all models by 1957, and there were various engine sizes. The most powerful carburettored version had a 270 bhp V8 engine and a top speed of 110 mph/176 kph. A fuel-injected 283 bhp version had a top speed of 120 mph/192 kph and up.

Engine	V8 4340 cc 162 bhp
Length	16 ft 5¹/₂ in/5 m
Width	6 ft 1 in/1.85 m
Top speed	103 mph/165 kph
Price new	$2229
Current	1950–76

Chevrolet Corvette Stingray

A brand-new Corvette appeared in 1963. It was called Sting Ray and featured pop-up headlights and a fuel-injected engine. The Sting Ray series compared very favourably with Britain's E Type Jaguar. A new-generation Corvette was produced in 1968, and the next year's model once again carried the name Stingray, this time written as one word.

Engine	V8 5736 cc 300 bhp
Length	15 ft 2 in/4.62 m
Width	5 ft 9 in/1.75 m
Top speed	124 mph/198 kph
Price new	$4763
Current	1963–77

Chrysler Airflow

Carl Breer's streamlined styling was first used on the bigger Chryslers and the 4 litre De Soto in 1934. The Airflow sported unitary construction, a waterfall grille and an alligator bonnet. Although the Chrysler could accelerate from 0–70 mph/112 kph in 26 seconds, difficulties with underbonnet accessibility, combined with unconventional looks, made the cars generally unpopular.

Engine	8 cylinder 4997 cc 125 bhp
Length	17 ft 4 in/5.28 m
Width	6 ft 4¼ in/1.94 m
Top speed	92 mph/147 kph
Price new	£595
Current	1934–37

Chrysler C300

The Chrysler C300 was the start of the famous Chrysler 300 series, and was one of America's first 'muscle cars'. Powered by Chrysler's V8 hemi-headed engine, the body was styled by Virgil Exner. The C300 was the world's most powerful car at the time of its introduction in 1955. Its advertising literature called it 'The Beautiful Brute'. The cars went on to compete successfully in NASCAR racing.

Engine	V8 5422 cc 300 bhp
Length	17 ft 11 in/5.46 m
Width	6 ft 7 in/2.01 m
Top speed	130 mph/208 kph
Price new	$4100
Current	1955–65

Citroën Traction Avant

When André Citroën put the Traction Avant into production in 1934, it was the world's first successful mass-produced front-wheel drive car. The design continued into the 1950s without much change. British versions were built at Slough. Three models were available towards the end of its production run. They were the Light 15, Big 15 and the Six, which had a six-cylinder 2866 cc engine.

Engine	4 cylinder 1911 cc 55.7 bhp
Length	14 ft 7 in/4.45 m
Width	5 ft 5¼ in/1.66 m
Top speed	75 mph/120 kph
Price new	£685
Current	1934–54

Citroën DS

The Citroën DS was a revolutionary car for its time, as it was very advanced both technically and in appearance. The initials DS caused the car to be affectionately known as the 'Deesse' or 'Goddess'. Many innovative features were incorporated into the car, among them hydropneumatic suspension, power steering and a single-spoke steering wheel. 0–60 mph/96 kph acceleration took 18.4 seconds.

Engine	4 cylinder 1911 cc 83 bhp
Length	15 ft 9 in/4.80 m
Width	5 ft 10¼ in/1.78 m
Top speed	91 mph/146 kph
Price new	£1630
Current	1955–75

Citroën SM

The Citroën SM was the product of an alliance with the Italian firm of Maserati. A sports coupé was designed by Citroën engineers and then fitted with a V6 Maserati engine. An unusual styling feature was a bank of six headlights set behind a glass screen. The car's performance figures were 0–60 mph/96 kph in 9.9 seconds and from a standing start to quarter of a mile/0.4 km in 17.4 seconds.

Engine	V6 2670 cc 170 bhp
Length	16 ft 0$\frac{1}{2}$ in/4.89 m
Width	6 ft 0$\frac{1}{2}$ in/1.84 m
Top speed	135 mph/216 kph
Price new	£5000
Current	1970–75

Citroën BX 19RD

Introduced in 1982, the BX was another individual design from Citroën. The car had features such as the revolving drum speedometer favoured by Citroën and a single windscreen wiper with four washer jets in the arm. Several engine sizes were offered, including the 19RD diesel. Fastest of the range was the 19 GTi, capable of 118 mph/189 kph.

Engine	4 cylinder 1905 cc 65 bhp
Length	13 ft 11 in/4.24 m
Width	5 ft 5 in/1.65 m
Top speed	97 mph/155 kph
Price new	£6314
Current	1982–94

Citroën 2CV

The Citroën 2CV was the 'people's car' of France. Developed before World War II, the first production car was manufactured in 1949. The 2CV was originally intended as a utility car for French agricultural workers. It has been described as an 'umbrella on wheels', but its shape and low fuel consumption won it worldwide popularity.

Engine	2 cylinder 602 cc 29 bhp
Length	12 ft 6 in/3.81 m
Width	4 ft 10 in/1.47 m
Top speed	68 mph/109 kph
Price new	£4116
Current	1949–90

Cord L29

The Cord L29 was similar to the more expensive Duesenberg in appearance. One of the earliest cars to feature front-wheel drive, the L29 had very good handling for such a large car. Unfortunately the steering was very heavy and required a great deal of effort at low speeds. Fitted with a straight-eight Lycoming engine, the Cord could accelerate from 0–60 mph/96 kph in 25 seconds.

Engine	8 cylinder 5175 cc 125 bhp
Length	16 ft 8 in/5.08 m
Width	6 ft/1.83 m
Top speed	75 mph/120 kph
Price new	£990
Current	1929–32

Cord 810 Sedan

Gordon Buehrig designed the Cord 810 for Erret Lobban Cord, who was also owner of Auburn and Duesenberg. Three models were offered: a four-door sedan, two-seater roadster and four-seater convertible coupé. All 810/812 models were nicknamed 'coffin nose'. An unusual feature was the headlamps, which could be raised by turning handles inside the car.

Engine	V8 4730 cc 125 bhp
Length	16 ft 3½ in/4.97 m
Width	5 ft 11 in/1.80 m
Top speed	102 mph/163 kph
Price new	£1025
Current	1936–37

Daimler

Daimler began manufacturing cars in Great Britain from 1896. A Daimler was one of the makes owned by King Edward VII. The car featured here was bought new by the present Lord Montagu of Beaulieu's father, John. This was the first car to be driven into the House of Commons yard, and the first all-British entry in a foreign road race.

Engine	4 cylinder 3053 cc
Length	10 ft 9 in/3.28 m
Width	5 ft 8 in/1.73 m
Top speed	30 mph/48 kph
Price new	£775
Current	1899–1900

Datsun 280ZX

Datsun added the 240Z sports car to its range in 1979. It quickly became one of the most popular sports cars. The 240Z also did well in competition events, and won the Safari Rally twice. A Targa top (detachable T-shaped roof) was an option on the later 280ZX series, and a further development was a turbo-charged version. In standard form the car could accelerate from 0–60 mph/96 kph in 10.1 seconds.

Engine	6 cylinder 2753 cc 140 bhp
Length	14 ft 3 in/4.34 m
Width	5 ft 6½ in/1.69 m
Top speed	111 mph/178 kph
Price new	£10,660
Current	1979–84

Delage GL

The French car company Delage was best known for its fast touring cars. In 1924 it offered its largest and most luxurious model – the GL. It was intended to rival such cars as the Isotta-Fraschini and Hispano-Suiza. The GL had servo-assisted brakes, an advanced feature of the period. The car illustrated appeared in the TV series *Brideshead Revisited* and the film *Chariots of Fire*.

Engine	6 cylinder 5954 cc 110 bhp
Length	16 ft 8 in/5.08 m
Width	5 ft 5 in/1.65 m
Top speed	80 mph/128 kph
Price new	£1100 chassis only
Current	1924–27

DeLorean

Founded by John DeLorean, the DeLorean Motor Company was based in Dunmurry, Northern Ireland. The car was styled by Giugiaro, had brushed stainless steel body panels and gullwing doors. The engine mounted in the rear was the Peugeot-Renault-Volvo 90 V6. A DeLorean car played an important role in the film *Back to the Future*.

Engine	V6 2849 cc 156 bhp
Length	14 ft/4.27 m
Width	6 ft/1.83 m
Top speed	112 mph/179 kph
Price new	$25,000
Current	1979–82

Dodge Six

Dodge was taken over by Chrysler in 1928. Both marques were assembled in Britain as well as America prior to World War II. Certain extras were fitted especially to appeal to the British market, and to make the cars appear more luxurious. Leather upholstery in the de luxe model was particularly popular. The Dodge Six had a six-cylinder side-valve engine, which could accelerate from 0–60 mph/96 kph in 24.8 seconds.

Engine	6 cylinder 3570 cc 71 bhp
Length	16 ft 5 in/5 m
Width	5 ft 10½ in/1.79 m
Top speed	80 mph/128 kph
Price new	£345
Current	1929–48

Dodge Charger 440 Magnum

The Dodge Charger was originally offered as a two-door sporting fastback. A change of company policy in 1967 saw the Charger emerge as a high-performance car. It went on to take part in several American TV series, *The Dukes of Hazzard* being one of them. A four-barrel carburettor was fitted as standard. The Dodge could accelerate to 60 mph/96 kph in 6.8 seconds.

Engine	V8 7207 cc 375 bhp
Length	17 ft 4 in/5.28 m
Width	6 ft 4½ in/1.94 m
Top speed	113 mph/181 kph
Price new	$3480
Current	1966–78

Duesenberg SJ

E.L. Cord of the Auburn Car Company took over Duesenberg in 1926. He insisted that the Duesenberg brothers should produce an exceptional car. The result was the fast and luxurious Model J, which was the most expensive mass-produced car at the time of its introduction. The SJ of 1932 was the supercharged version. It was claimed that the SJ could accelerate from 0–100 mph/160 kph in 17 seconds.

Engine	8 cylinder 6882 cc 320 bhp
Length	17 ft 6 in/5.33 m
Width	6 ft/1.83 m
Top speed	120 mph/192 kph
Price new	£3500
Current	1929–37

Ferrari 166

Enzo Ferrari began producing sports cars with the intro-duction of the Type 166. The cars took part in road racing from the very start, and a 166 driven by Biondetti won the Mille Miglia in 1948. The V12 engine was designed by Giochino Colombo, and the famous Barchetta body was styled by Touring of Milan.

Engine	V12 1995 cc 130 bhp
Length	13 ft 2 in/4 m
Width	4 ft 3½ in/1.31 m
Top speed	100 mph/160 kph
Price new	N/A
Current	1947–53

Ferrari 365 Daytona

Ferrari sports cars evolved into exotic performance cars in the 1970s and 80s. The Daytona was the most comfortable and luxurious in the range. The car was fitted with servo disc brakes, and was unusual in that the gearbox and back axle were in the same unit. Acceleration from 0–60 mph/96 kph took the Daytona 5.4 seconds. The standing start to quarter of a mile/0.4 km took 13.7 seconds.

Engine	V12 4390 cc 352 bhp
Length	14 ft 6 in/4.42 m
Width	5 ft 9 in/1.75 m
Top speed	174 mph/278 kph
Price new	£9572
Current	1969–74

Ferrari Testarossa

The Pininfarina-designed Ferrari Testarossa influenced many other car stylists of the mid-1980s. The things most copied were the Testarossa side air intakes. Mechanically the car was based on a multi-tubular space frame, and the engine unit was very similar to the company's earlier Boxer engine. At the time of introduction the Testarossa was the world's fastest production car. 0–60 mph/96 kph took 5.2 seconds.

Engine	V12 4942 cc 390 bhp
Length	14 ft 8½ in/4.48 m
Width	6 ft 6 in/1.98 m
Top speed	171 mph/274 kph
Price new	£62,666
Current	1984–91

Ferrari F40

Enzo Ferrari produced the F40 in 1987 as a celebration of 40 years of Ferrari cars. It was originally intended to produce a limited edition run of 450 cars. However, Ferrari management decided that the model should continue as long as there was a demand for it. The power unit was a rear-engined 32-valve V8 with twin turbo-chargers. 0–124 mph/198 kph took just 12 seconds.

Engine	V8 2963 cc 478 bhp
Length	14 ft 6$\frac{1}{2}$ in/4.43 m
Width	6 ft 6 in/1.98 m
Top speed	201 mph/322 kph
Price new	£200,000
Current	1987–92

Fiat 500

The little Fiat 500 Topolino was affectionately known as 'Mickey Mouse' by its many admirers. It was designed by Dante Giacosa, and, despite its 6 ft 6 in wheelbase, could seat two adults and two small children. Fiat 500s handled well, and the cars proved surprisingly popular at rallies and hill-climbs, even if it did take 63.6 seconds to reach 50 mph/80 kph.

Engine	4 cylinder 570 cc 13 bhp
Length	10 ft 8½ in/3.26 m
Width	4 ft 3½ in/1.31 m
Top speed	49 mph/78 kph
Price new	£120
Current	1936–55

Fiat Dino

Ferrari approached Fiat and asked if it would collaborate in designing a Fiat sports car powered by a Ferrari V6 Dino engine. This strategy would enable Ferrari to have 5000 road cars powered by its V6 engine, making the cars eligible for racing. Fiat agreed and the result was the open two-seater Fiat Dino. A coupé version by Bertone was produced a little later.

Engine	V6 2418 cc 180 bhp
Length	13 ft 7 in/4.14 m
Width	5 ft 7 in/1.70 m
Top speed	129 mph/206 kph
Price new	£3490
Current	1967–72

Ford Model T

One of the most significant models in motoring history, the Ford Model T sold at an exceptionally low price to millions of people throughout the world. The Model T was the first car to be assembled on a moving production line. Over 16 million were built. Henry Ford's 'Tin Lizzie' was also known as the 'Flivver'. 0–40 mph/64 kph took 32.9 seconds.

Engine	4 cylinder 2898 cc 20 bhp
Length	11 ft 2 in/3.40 m
Width	5 ft 10½ in/1.79 m
Top speed	40 mph/64 kph
Price new	£135
Current	1909–27

Ford Model A

Henry Ford closed down his factory for six months in 1927 while he changed over from producing the Model T to the Model A. The Model A had the more conventional layout of the two, with a three-speed gearbox and four-wheel brakes. The body was similar in styling to the Lincoln, a company which Ford also owned. 0–40 mph/64 kph was reached in 23 seconds.

Engine	4 cylinder 2033 cc 28 bhp
Length	12 ft 7½ in/3.85 m
Width	5 ft 7 in/1.70 m
Top speed	55 mph/88 kph
Price new	£185
Current	1927–31

Ford V8

Ford offered one of the first mass-produced cars to be fitted with a low-priced V8 engine. This was in 1932. By 1935 the Ford V8 had become a bestseller and had sold a million. A single downdraught carburettor was fitted to the cast-iron V8 engine, which was capable of propelling the car from 0–50 mph/80 kph in 26 seconds.

Engine	V8 3630 cc 65 bhp
Length	13 ft 9½ in/4.20 m
Width	5 ft 6½ in/1.69 m
Top speed	75 mph/120 kph
Price new	£255
Current	1932–54

Ford Model Y

Ford of Great Britain introduced the Model Y in 1933. At the time it was the first full-size saloon car to sell for £100 in Britain. The Model Y was also the first Ford to be developed solely for sale in Britain to rival Morris and Austin. The great advantage that the Model Y had was its synchronized gearbox. 0–50 mph/80 kph took 24 seconds.

Engine	4 cylinder 933 cc 22 bhp
Length	11 ft 11 in/3.63 m
Width	4 ft 6 in/1.37 m
Top speed	62 mph/99 kph
Price new	£100
Current	1933–37

Ford Anglia

For 29 years Ford used the name Anglia, but on four different cars. The first one appeared in 1939 and continued until 1948, when the second series was produced. This model had a smoother front end and no running boards. Later 1952–59 Anglias had an 1172 cc engine and streamlined body. The final version was the 105E, with a 933 cc overhead valve engine and angular body design.

Engine	4 cylinder 933 cc 23.4 bhp
Length	12 ft 8 in/3.86 m
Width	4 ft 8 in/1.42 m
Top speed	60 mph/96 kph
Price new	£309
Current	1939–68

Ford Consul

The first postwar cars to come from the British Ford factory at Dagenham were almost identical to prewar models. Two completely new designs appeared in 1951: the Ford Consul and Consul Convertible. The Consul became very popular with fleet users and company management. As only 3750 Convertibles were produced, the model was always rare.

Engine	4 cylinder 1508 cc 47 bhp
Length	13 ft 6½ in/4.13 m
Width	5 ft 4 in/1.63 m
Top speed	75 mph/120 kph
Price new	£853
Current	1951–56

Ford Thunderbird

Ford intended the Thunderbird to fill the gap in the luxury 'personal' car market. At the time most cars manufactured in America were full-size saloons. The Thunderbird was a two-seater when first produced. It later became a full four-seater. The 245 bhp version had a single four-barrel carburettor and a 0–60 mph/96 kph time of 7.4 seconds.

Engine	V8 5117 cc 245 bhp
Length	15 ft 1 in/4.60 m
Width	6 ft 1 in/1.85 m
Top speed	112 mph/179 kph
Price new	£2771
Current	1954–83

Ford Zephyr Mk II

Ford's six-cylinder Zephyr and Zodiac, together with the four-cylinder Consul, made up the company's large-car range of the 1950s and early 60s. The Mk II range was announced in 1956. Lowered body lines and a redesigned radiator grille were the model's chief distinguishing features. Disc brakes became standard in 1960. 0–60 mph/96 kph took 16.5 seconds.

Engine	6 cylinder 2553 cc 85 bhp
Length	14 ft 11 in/4.55 m
Width	5 ft 8 in/1.73 m
Top speed	90 mph/144 kph
Price new	£865
Current	1956–62

Ford Cortina Mk I

Ford launched the Cortina Mk I in 1962. It was named after the famous Italian ski resort. Instantly popular, the Cortina offered comfortable transport for five people and their luggage, all at a small-car price. Acceleration from 0–60 mph/96 kph took 22.5 seconds. Ford Cortinas were successful company and hire vehicles. A Lotus Cortina appeared in 1963 powered by a Lotus-tuned engine.

Engine	4 cylinder 1198 cc 53 bhp
Length	14 ft 2$^{1}/_{2}$ in/4.33 m
Width	5 ft 3 in/1.60 m
Top speed	80 mph/128 kph
Price new	£639
Current	1962–66

Ford Mustang

The Ford Mustang was the Ford Motor Company's sporting car of the 1960s. It was marketed mainly with young drivers in mind. Lee Iococca promoted it so successfully that over 400,000 units were sold in one year. There were several engine sizes and interior options. One of the most powerful was the 271 bhp V8, and the smallest was a six-cylinder 101 bhp.

Engine	V8 4261 cc 271 bhp
Length	15 ft 1^1/$_2$ in/4.61 m
Width	5 ft 8^1/$_2$ in/1.74 m
Top speed	111 mph/178 kph
Price new	$2368
Current	1964–present

Ford Escort Mk I TC

Ford of Great Britain replaced the 105E Anglia with the Mk I Escort in 1968. A small family car, there were several different models to choose from. The 'hottest' version was the Escort Twin Cam, which could accelerate from 0–60 mph/96 kph in under 10 seconds. The Works cars had numerous competition wins, including the International Tulip Rally and Thousand Lakes Rally.

Engine	4 cylinder 1588 cc 115 bhp
Length	13 ft 4 in/4.06 m
Width	5 ft 1³/₄ in/1.57 m
Top speed	112 mph/179 kph
Price new	£1195
Current	1968–75

Ford Escort RS1600i

RS are the initials of Rallye Sport. Ford had made a practice of producing competition saloons since the days of the Mk I Escort. In road-going form the cars were popular, affordable performance cars. The RS1600i was unusual in that it had front-wheel drive, combined with the comfort of the Ford XR3. Bosch fuel injection was fitted as standard. 0–60 mph/96 kph took 8.7 seconds.

Engine	4 cylinder 1596 cc 115 bhp
Length	13 ft 3¹/₂ in/4.05 m
Width	5 ft 2¹/₂ in/1.59 m
Top speed	116 mph/186 kph
Price new	£6834
Current	1983–89

Gilbern Invader

Welsh car-maker Gilbern was responsible for the V6-engined Invader. Designed to be a GT car, the Invader was a revised edition of the Gilbern Genie. The car featured a fibreglass body, aluminium wheels and optional overdrive. Power was by the same engine unit as in the Ford Zodiac. 0–60 mph/96 kph took 10.7 seconds. A few estate versions were made.

Engine	V6 2994 cc 141 bhp
Length	13 ft 3 in/4.04 m
Width	5 ft 5 in/1.65 m
Top speed	115 mph/185 kph
Price new	£2412
Current	1969–73

Gordon Keeble

Named after John Gordon and Jim Keeble, the Gordon Keeble was powered by the same engine as the Chevrolet Corvette. Body design was by Giugiaro and made of fibreglass. The car was fitted with disc brakes and a telescopic steering wheel. Although the Gordon Keeble was well liked by the motoring press, only 99 were sold. 0–60 mph/96 kph took 7.5 seconds.

Engine	V8 5355 cc 300 bhp
Length	15 ft 9½ in/4.81 m
Width	5 ft 8 in/1.73 m
Top speed	135 mph/216 kph
Price new	£3627
Current	1964–66

Healey 2.4

Donald Healey was a successful prewar rally driver, who manufactured his first production car in 1946. The Healey 2.4 was available as a saloon or roadster. Both models were successful rally cars, winning class victories in the 1947 and 1948 Alpine rallies. Healey himself competed with a 2.4 in the Mille Miglia and came ninth. 0–60 mph/96 kph took 14.7 seconds.

Engine	4 cylinder 2443 cc 104 bhp
Length	14 ft/4.27 m
Width	5 ft 5½ in/1.66 m
Top speed	104 mph/166 kph
Price new	£1598
Current	1946–50

Healey Silverstone

Donald Healey produced the first two-seater Healey Silverstone in 1949. Its chassis was based on that of the Healey Saloon, but with a shortened frame. The Silverstone also featured shorter springs and an anti-roll bar. Power was from a 2.5 litre four-cylinder Riley engine, which was then married to a light alloy body.

Engine	4 cylinder 2443 cc 104 bhp
Length	14 ft/4.27 m
Width	5 ft 3 in/1.60 m
Top speed	100 mph/160 kph
Price new	£975
Current	1949–50

Heinkel Cabin Cruiser

Fears of petrol shortages in the 1950s led to a proliferation of bubble cars. Aircraft manufacturers Heinkel originally produced the Cabin Cruiser, while Trojan produced them in Great Britain from 1961. The Cabin Cruiser managed an amazing average petrol consumption of 90 mpg, and had enough space for two adults and two children.

Engine	1 cylinder 198 cc 13 bhp
Length	9 ft 1 in/2.77 m
Width	4 ft 9 in/1.45 m
Top speed	60 mph/96 kph
Price new	£389
Current	1955–65

Hillman Minx

Hillman produced its first compact family car in 1931, and was one of the first manufacturers to offer a radio as an option in the Melody Minx of 1934. The series IIIC of 1961 was very similar to the Singer Gazelle and Sunbeam Rapier. The engine was slightly larger than the previous model, giving a 0–60 mph/96 kph time of 16.1 seconds.

Engine	4 cylinder 1592 cc 52.8 bhp
Length	13 ft 6½ in/4.13 m
Width	5 ft 1 in/1.55 m
Top speed	78 mph/124 kph
Price new	£702
Current	1961–63

Hillman Imp

Intended to rival the ever-popular Mini, the Hillman Imp was made at Linwood in Scotland. The Imp was powered by a rear-engined Coventry Climax unit of 875 cc, with a single overhead camshaft. Roadhandling was excellent and the Imp was comfortable by small-car standards. 0–50 mph/80 kph took 14.9 seconds. The range included saloon, estate and coupé versions.

Engine	4 cylinder 875 cc 39 bhp
Length	11 ft 7 in/3.53 m
Width	5 ft 0$\frac{1}{2}$ in/1.54 m
Top speed	78 mph/124 kph
Price new	£532
Current	1963–76

Hispano-Suiza Alfonso

Hispano-Suiza named its Edwardian sports car after the company's most illustrious client, King Alfonso XIII. The Alfonso was developed to take part in early long-distance endurance rallies like the Prince Henry, Herkomer and 1000 mile trials. The Hispano was similar to a current sports car in that it was quite short in length and close to the ground.

Engine	4 cylinder 3615 cc 15 HP
Length	12 ft 4^1/$_2$ in/3.77 m
Width	5 ft 4^1/$_2$ in/1.64 m
Top speed	75 mph/120 kph
Price new	£545
Current	1909–16

Hispano-Suiza H6C

Hispano-Suizas were produced in France from 1911. The first French-designed Hispano was the H6. The H6 model chassis was bodied by many fashionable coach-builders. One of the most unique was the Torpedo Tulipwood tourer pictured here, built by Nieuport Astra. Marc Birkigt designed the overhead valve engine, which the makers recommended should be cruised at 50 mph/80 kph.

Engine	6 cylinder 6597 cc 135 bhp
Length	15 ft 5½ in/4.71 m
Width	5 ft 3 in/1.60 m
Top speed	75 mph/120 kph
Price new	£1500 chassis only
Current	1919–33

Hispano-Suiza 45

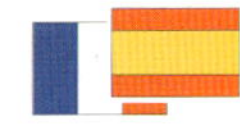

Manufactured in both France and Spain, the Hispano-Suiza was a favourite luxury car, particularly in France. The chassis was bodied by many of the finest coach-builders of the day; illustrated is an example of a boat-tail body. Two engine sizes were offered for sale in 1928. The larger 45 HP was the sports model, with a top speed of 95 mph/152 kph.

Engine	6 cylinder 7892 cc 45 HP
Length	14 ft 10 in/4.52 m
Width	5 ft 9½ in/1.77 m
Top speed	95 mph/152 kph
Price new	£1950
Current	1919–34

Honda S800

Motorcycle manufacturer Honda developed a two-seater sports car to rival the Triumph Spitfire and MG Midget. It was exported in 1967 as the S800, and proved to be very powerful for such a small sports car, having a twin overhead camshaft engine that could spin at 8000 rpm. 0–60 mph/96 kph took 13.6 seconds.

Engine	4 cylinder 791 cc 70 bhp
Length	10 ft 11½ in/3.33 m
Width	4 ft 7¼ in/1.40 m
Top speed	94 mph/150 kph
Price new	£779
Current	1965–70

Horch V12

Horch was founded by August Horch, who left the company in 1909 to form Audi. The Horch car company went on, under Paul Daimler, to produce luxury cars that could rival Mercedes-Benz. In 1930 the company launched its first V12, with a choice of two wheelbase sizes. The V12 was fitted with a four-speed synchromesh gearbox.

Engine	V12 5990 cc 120 bhp
Length	17 ft 8½ in/5.40 m
Width	5 ft 11 in/1.80 m
Top speed	85 mph/136 kph
Price new	N/A
Current	1930–32

Hotchkiss

Hotchkiss competed very successfully in the Monte Carlo Rally, scoring wins in 1932, 1933, 1934 and 1939, and three successive postwar wins in 1948, 1949 and 1950. The engine of the 3.5 litre cars, known as the Paris-Nice, was a pushrod-operated overhead cam unit helped by twin carburettors. Production of Hotchkiss cars ceased after a merger with Delahaye.

Engine	6 cylinder 3485 cc 95 bhp
Length	16 ft 1 in/4.90 m
Width	5 ft 10 in/1.78 m
Top speed	95 mph/152 kph
Price new	N/A
Current	1950–54

Invicta 4.5 Litre

Invicta, producer of fast touring cars, was founded by Noel Macklin and Oliver Lyle of the famous company Tate & Lyle. An Invicta won the Monte Carlo Rally in 1931. Violet Cordery drove another Invicta around the world. Invicta offered the 4.5 litre model in two versions, a high chassis and low chassis model, with an underslung rear frame.

Engine	6 cylinder 4467 cc 100 bhp
Length	14 ft 4 in/4.37 m
Width	5 ft 6 in/1.68 m
Top speed	90 mph/144 kph
Price new	£950
Current	1931–35

Isotta Fraschini Tipo 8A

Isotta Fraschini straight eights were luxury chauffeur-driven cars, popular with American film stars. An 8A featured in the film *Sunset Boulevard*. Isotta equipped the 8A with servo-assisted brakes in 1925, but the cars were still enormously heavy to steer. A sports version, the 8ASS, had a power output of 135 bhp and a top speed of 104 mph/166 kph.

Engine	8 cylinder 7372 cc 120 bhp
Length	16 ft 4 in/4.98 m
Width	5 ft 8 in/1.73 m
Top speed	90 mph/144 kph
Price new	£1750
Current	1925–31

Itala 120 HP

Itala was one of the leading Italian quality car-makers before World War I. In 1907 the company entered three cars for the Coppa della Velocita Race at Brescia. The team finished first, eighth and tenth. The winning car was driven by Cagno at an average speed of 65 mph/104 kph for 302 miles/483 km.

Engine	4 cylinder 14432 cc 120 HP
Length	13 ft 6 in/4.11 m
Width	5 ft 6 in/1.68 m
Top speed	100 mph/160 kph
Price new	N/A
Current	1907

Jaguar SS100

William Lyons used the name Jaguar for the first time in 1936. After World War II the SS part of the name was dropped entirely. The SS100 was much admired for its flowing good looks and performance at a reasonable price. The engine was made by the Standard Motor Company, but with modifications by Weslake and Heynes.

Engine	6 cylinder 2664 cc 104 bhp
Length	13 ft 1 in/3.99 m
Width	5 ft 3 in/1.60 m
Top speed	95 mph/152 kph
Price new	£395
Current	1936–39

Jaguar XK120

William Lyons designed a smooth aerodynamic body style for the Jaguar XK120. This represented a great advance in car styling in the late 40s, and influenced many other car-makers. Many XK120s were made for export to America. Power came from a twin overhead-camshaft unit, the first engine that Jaguar itself produced.

Engine	6 cylinder 3442 cc 160 bhp
Length	14 ft 5$\frac{1}{2}$ in/4.41 m
Width	5 ft 2 in/1.57 m
Top speed	120 mph/192 kph
Price new	£1130
Current	1949–54

Jaguar 3.4 Mk II

The Mk II series of Jaguars were externally different from the earlier Mk Is in that they had thicker bumpers and a wrap-round rear window. Intended to be Jaguar's medium-sized saloons, the cars came with a choice of 2.4, 3.4 and 3.8 litre engines. Power steering was an optional extra. Several branches of the police used them as patrol vehicles.

Engine	6 cylinder 3442 cc 210 bhp
Length	15 ft 1 in/4.60 m
Width	5 ft 7 in/1.70 m
Top speed	120 mph/192 kph
Price new	£1619
Current	1959–68

Jaguar E Type

Another revolutionary shape for Jaguar was the E Type of 1961, which came equipped with all-round servo-assisted disc brakes and independent front suspension. As with Jaguar's earlier XK series, the E Type proved popular in America. The basic design continued into the mid-70s, and by then a V12 engine was available as an option.

Engine	6 cylinder 3781 cc 265 bhp
Length	14 ft 7 in/4.45 m
Width	5 ft 5½ in/1.66 m
Top speed	150 mph/240 kph
Price new	£2160
Current	1961–75

Jaguar XJ220

In 1992 the XJ220 was the fastest and most expensive car in the world. Originally the car was displayed at the 1988 Birmingham Motor Show, but did not go into production for another four years. It was during this time that Ford took over Jaguar. The mid-engined V6 engine had electronic multi-point fuel injection and a bore/stroke of 94/84 mm. 0–60 mph/96 kph acceleration was 3.75 seconds.

Engine	V6 3500 cc 542 bhp
Length	16 ft 2 in/4.93 m
Width	7 ft 3½ in/2.22 m
Top speed	212 mph/339 kph
Price new	£415,544
Current	1992–93

Jensen Interceptor

Jensen was a company which had many motoring 'firsts' to its credit. Among them were four-wheel drive on the FF, and a full-size saloon in fibreglass with the CV8 and 541 models. The Interceptor was styled by Touring, with early cars built by Vignale. Powered by an American Chrysler V8 engine, the Interceptor could accelerate from 0–60 mph/96 kph in 6.4 seconds.

Engine	8 cylinder 6276 cc 330 bhp
Length	15 ft 8 in/4.78 m
Width	5 ft 10 in/1.78 m
Top speed	137 mph/219 kph
Price new	£5198
Current	1966–76

Jowett Javelin

Jowett produced this saloon and a sports car, the Jowett Jupiter, in the 1950s. The models were very advanced for their day, which may have contributed to the company failing in 1954. Styling of the saloon car was influenced by American car design. Both Jowetts were powered by a horizontally-opposed flat four engine.

Engine	4 cylinder 1486 cc 50 bhp
Length	14 ft 10 in/4.52 m
Width	5 ft 1 in/1.55 m
Top speed	80 mph/128 kph
Price new	£675
Current	1947–53

Lagonda 2 Litre

Lagonda produced its first proper sports car in 1927. Known as the 2 litre Speed Model, it was highly praised by the motoring press of the day. Later cars had a lowered chassis, and a supercharged version was available from 1930. An early road test of the Speed Model quotes a top speed of nearly 80 mph/128 kph and a 0–70 mph/112 kph acceleration time of 60 seconds.

Engine	4 cylinder 1954 cc 75 bhp
Length	14 ft 3 in/4.34 m
Width	5 ft 7 in/1.70 m
Top speed	75 mph/120 kph
Price new	£695
Current	1927–32

Lagonda V12

The V12 Lagonda was designed by W.O. Bentley, who went to work for Lagonda after the collapse of Bentley Motors. The V12 engine is said by many to be the finest that Bentley ever produced in terms of flexibility and performance. A Lagonda DeVille saloon lapped Brooklands at 101 mph/161 kph, a great feat for such a large saloon car.

Engine	V12 4480 cc 180 bhp
Length	16 ft 2 in/5.23 m
Width	6 ft/1.83 m
Top speed	101 mph/161 kph
Price new	£1625
Current	1937–39

Lagonda 2.6

Lagonda was bought by David Brown in 1947 and subsequently became part of Aston Martin. The 2.6 litre was W.O. Bentley's last design. The car was produced with a twin OHC engine, all-independent springing and column gear change. A later version, the 3.2 litre, was introduced in 1951. The Duke of Edinburgh owned two.

Engine	6 cylinder 2580 cc 105 bhp
Length	15 ft 8 in/4.77 m
Width	5 ft 8 in/1.72 m
Top speed	76 mph/122 kph
Price new	£2250
Current	1948–53

Lamborghini Countach

Lamborghini has been making fast and stylish supercars since 1964. The Countach (pronounced 'Coontash') was one of the most memorable. Marcello Gandini of Bertone was responsible for styling, featuring upward-opening doors hinged at the front. Acceleration times were the fastest of the period: 0–60 mph/96 kph took 5.6 seconds, and a standing start to quarter of a mile/0.4 km took 14.1 seconds.

Engine	V12 3929 cc 375 bhp
Length	13 ft 7 in/4.14 m
Width	6 ft 2$^{1}/_{2}$ in/1.89 m
Top speed	175 mph/280 kph
Price new	£16,314
Current	1973–90

Lamborghini Diablo

The Lamborghini Countach ceased production in 1990 and was replaced by the Diablo. Marcello Gandini was again appointed by Lamborghini as stylist of the new car, although by now Lamborghini was part of Chrysler. The Diablo was designed with a larger engine and twin catalytic converters. The world's fastest four-wheel drive production car is the Diablo VT, capable of 0–60 mph/96 kph in 5.1 seconds.

Engine	V12 5709 cc 492 bhp
Length	14 ft 8 in/4.47 m
Width	6 ft 8 in/2.03 m
Top speed	202 mph/323 kph
Price new	£143,937
Current	1990–present

Lanchester 20 HP

Brothers George and Frederick Lanchester designed their first car in 1895 and went into production in 1900. Frederick was responsible for several advanced technical innovations, including disc brakes and a semi-automatic gearbox. The 1908 Lanchester 20 HP had tiller steering, three-speed semi-epicyclic gearbox and a hand-operated clutch. Later models had steering wheels.

Engine	4 cylinder 2470 cc 20 HP
Length	13 ft/3.96 m
Width	5 ft 9 in/1.75 m
Top speed	50 mph/80 kph
Price new	£500 chassis only
Current	1905–11

Lanchester 10 HP

BSA, which already owned Daimler, bought Lanchester in 1931. From then on Lanchester produced smaller family cars. Although the 10 was the least powerful of the range, it gave a smooth ride and was very comfortable. Lanchester 10s had a fluid flywheel and pre-selector gearbox fitted as standard. 0–50 mph/80 kph took 29 seconds.

Engine	4 cylinder 1444 cc 10.8 HP
Length	13 ft 3¼ in/4.04 m
Width	4 ft 10 in/1.47 m
Top speed	62 mph/99 kph
Price new	£298
Current	1933–37

Lancia Lambda

Vincenzo Lancia produced the first Lambda in 1922. It was a remarkable car for its time, having unitary construction and independent front suspension. It was a highly thought-of touring car with sporting characteristics. The Lambda survived into its ninth series, 13,000 being produced in all. Acceleration from 10–30 mph/48 kph took 6 seconds.

Engine	4 cylinder 2570 cc 69 bhp
Length	13 ft 5 in/4.09 m
Width	5 ft 6 in/1.68 m
Top speed	70 mph/112 kph
Price new	£745
Current	1922–31

Lancia Aprilia

Lancia introduced the Aprilia in 1937; it was the last design to be created by Vincenzo Lancia, the firm's founder. The Aprilia was streamlined in appearance, and had such good handling that it could be called one of the first small sporting saloons. The model was so successful that it stayed in postwar production for three years. 0–60 mph/96 kph acceleration took 25.2 seconds.

Engine	4 cylinder 1352 cc 47 bhp
Length	13 ft 7½ in/4.15 m
Width	4 ft 10 in/1.47 m
Top speed	80 mph/128 kph
Price new	£330
Current	1937–49

Lancia Fulvia

Lancia launched the front-wheel drive Fulvia in 1965 as a replacement for the Appia. The model was offered as a saloon or coupé on a shortened wheelbase. Fulvias soon became active in sports-car racing. They competed in events like the RAC Rally and East African Safari. A Zagato-bodied sports car was also produced. 0–60 mph/96 kph took the Fulvia 15.8 seconds.

Engine	V4 1298 cc 85 bhp
Length	13 ft 0$^{1}/_{2}$ in/3.98 m
Width	5 ft 2 in/1.57 m
Top speed	100 mph/160 kph
Price new	£1490
Current	1965–76

Lancia Thema LX Turbo

Lancia and Saab collaborated to produce the Lancia Thema and Saab 9000. This saved on development costs, but there were very few components common to both cars. The LX Turbo was a more luxurious version of the Thema ie Turbo, but both featured a Garrett T3 supercharger and Bosch LE-2 fuel injection. 0–60 mph/96 kph took 7.6 seconds.

Engine	4 cylinder 1995 cc 165 bhp
Length	15 ft 0³/₄ in/4.59 m
Width	5 ft 10 in/1.78 m
Top speed	139 mph/222 kph
Price new	£17,995
Current	1985–89

Land Rover Discovery

The Land Rover Discovery is one of the few vehicles to successfully combine the two functions of people-carrier and off-road vehicle. It is cheaper than a Range Rover but more luxurious than a Defender, with an interior designed by Conran. Petrol and turbo diesel versions are available. The fuel-injected V8 can accelerate from 0–60 mph/96 kph in 11.7 seconds.

Engine	V8 3528 cc 164 bhp
Length	14 ft 10 in/4.52 m
Width	5 ft 10$\frac{1}{2}$ in/1.79 m
Top speed	105 mph/168 kph
Price new	£17,776
Current	1989–present

Lincoln Continental

Lincoln is a subsidiary of the Ford Motor Company, and produces cars aimed at the luxury market. The Lincoln Continental appeared as a model in its own right in 1941. Mechanically, the Lincoln Continental was the same as the cheaper Lincoln Zephyr. Ford fitted column gear change for the first time ever on the '41 Continental model.

Engine	V12 5018 cc 120 bhp
Length	17 ft 6 in/5.33 m
Width	6 ft 1 in/1.85 m
Top speed	101 mph/161 kph
Price new	$2622
Current	1941–present

Lotus Elite

The Lotus Elite was Colin Chapman's first production road-going car. Constructed of fibreglass, it was also known as the Lotus 14. Lotus offered the Elite as a complete car or in kit form ready to assemble. The car's suspension featured Chapman-designed rear struts. Series 2 Elites were given an all-synchromesh gearbox and a larger engine.

Engine	4 cylinder 1216 cc 75 bhp
Length	12 ft 6 in/3.81 m
Width	4 ft 10 in/1.47 m
Top speed	115 mph/184 kph
Price new	£1948
Current	1958–63

Lotus Esprit Turbo

A second series of the Lotus Esprit Turbo was launched in 1980, possessing superb looks and performance that put it firmly in the Ferrari and Porsche class. The difference was that it was at a much lower price. The Esprit is powered by an all-alloy 16-valve twin-cam engine, fitted with a Garrett turbocharger. 0–60 mph/96 kph acceleration takes 5 seconds.

Engine	4 cylinder 2174 cc 214 bhp
Length	14 ft 2½ in/4.33 m
Width	6 ft 1 in/1.85 m
Top speed	153 mph/245 kph
Price new	£29,950
Current	1980–present

Lotus Esprit S4

Lotus produced its first Esprit Turbo in 1980. Colin Chapman, the company's founder, died in 1982. The firm was taken over by General Motors in 1986, which later sold it to Bugatti. The latest evolution of the Esprit is the S4, launched at the Geneva Motor Show in March 1993. This model features a 300 bhp all-aluminium alloy 16-valve engine.

Engine	4 cylinder 2174 cc 264 bhp
Length	14 ft 4 in/4.37 m
Width	6 ft 1$\frac{1}{2}$ in/1.87 m
Top speed	160 mph/256 kph
Price new	£46,995
Current	1993–present

Marcos 3 Litre

Designed by the Adams brothers, the Marcos was one of the first hardtop two-seater sports cars. Powered by a V6 Ford Zephyr engine, the 3 litre was based on the smaller-engined 1600 Marcos, suitably modified to take the larger engine and gearbox. The bodywork was fibreglass. 0–60 mph/96 kph took 7.8 seconds. A Volvo engine later replaced the Ford unit.

Engine	V6 2994 cc 141 bhp
Length	13 ft 4$^{1}/_{4}$ in/4.07 m
Width	5 ft 2$^{1}/_{4}$ in/1.58 m
Top speed	125 mph/200 kph
Price new	£2350
Current	1968–72

Maserati Merak SS

Maserati introduced the Merak as a lower priced alternative to the V8-engined Bora. The mid-engined Merak was styled by Giugiaro. Power came from the same engine as the Citroën SM, a car which had been developed by Citroën and Maserati. Fitted with three carburettors, the Merak SS could accelerate from 0–60 mph/96 kph in 7.7 seconds.

Engine	6 cylinder 2963 cc 208 bhp
Length	14 ft 2$\frac{1}{2}$ in/4.33 m
Width	5 ft 3 in/1.60 m
Top speed	143 mph/229 kph
Price new	£23,261
Current	1972–81

Maserati Ghibli

The original Ghibli was introduced in 1967, Maserati deciding to use the name again on one of its new 1994 models. Based on the Bi-Turbo shape, the Ghibli has a 24-valve twin-turbo V6 engine. The body style of the latest Ghibli has been criticized when compared to earlier Maseratis. The performance figures and price compare well to Ferrari and Lamborghini. 0–60 mph/96 kph acceleration takes 5.6 seconds.

Engine	V6 2790 cc 280 bhp
Length	14 ft 4$^1/_2$ in/4.38 m
Width	5 ft 10 in/1.78 m
Top speed	153 mph/245 kph
Price new	£43,816
Current	1994–present

Mazda RX7

Mazda is one of the few firms to successfully market cars with rotary engines. It offered its first twin Wankel rotary engine in a sports coupé of 1967. The Mazda RX7 followed in 1978. The car was intended to compete with the Porsche 924 and Lotus Eclat. 0–60 mph/96 kph took 10.1 seconds. A twin turbo-charged convertible was introduced in 1991.

Engine	twin rotors 2292 cc 105 bhp
Length	14 ft 1 in/4.29 m
Width	5 ft 6 in/1.68 m
Top speed	113 mph/181 kph
Price new	£9199
Current	1978–present

Mazda MX5

When Mazda introduced its MX5, the motoring press loved it. Several journalists reported that it was the sort of small two-seater sports car that Britain should be making badged as an MG. The bodywork is very similar to the old-style Lotus Elan. Power comes from a twin-camshaft 16-valve engine. 0–60 mph/96 kph acceleration time is 9.1 seconds.

Engine	4 cylinder 1598 cc 114 bhp
Length	13 ft 1 in/3.99 m
Width	5 ft 6 in/1.68 m
Top speed	114 mph/182 kph
Price new	£15,299
Current	1990–present

McLaren F1

Gordon Murray and Peter Stevens of McLaren began work developing the fastest supercar in the world in 1989. The F1 has an unorthodox seating arrangement, in that the driver sits in the centre of the car and the passengers either side. A 48-valve V12 BMW engine powers the car linked to a six-speed gearbox.

Engine	V12 6064 cc 627 bhp
Length	14 ft 1 in/4.29 m
Width	6 ft/1.83 m
Top speed	231 mph/370 kph
Price new	£540,000
Current	1993–present

Mercedes-Benz SSK

The Mercedes-Benz SSK sports cars were designed by Ferdinand Porsche. Fitted with a supercharger, the unit was designed to be immensely powerful yet flexible. This in turn made the cars very successful in competition events. The factory-fitted body was very stylish, but some owners preferred to have their cars bodied by coach-builders such as Corsica and Saoutchik.

Engine	6 cylinder 7069 cc 225 bhp
Length	15 ft 9 in/4.80 m
Width	5 ft 8 in/1.73 m
Top speed	115 mph/184 kph
Price new	£2150
Current	1928–32

Mercedes-Benz 300SL Gullwing

The Mercedes-Benz 300SL, with its gullwing doors hinged in the roof, is perhaps the best known of the 300SL series. It was also one of the first mass-produced cars to be fitted with fuel injection. Only left-hand drive versions were made. The hinged steering wheel helped with access to the driving seat. 0–60 mph/96 kph took 8.9 seconds.

Engine	6 cylinder 2996 cc 240 bhp
Length	14 ft 7 in/4.45 m
Width	5 ft 10 in/1.78 m
Top speed	140 mph/224 kph
Price new	£3100
Current	1954–58

Mercedes-Benz 190

Mercedes-Benz launched the 190 in 1983; it was the company's first small car for some time. Although the 190 did not have many accessories fitted as standard, buyers were assured of the usual Mercedes-Benz reputation for build quality. The standard 190 was able to accelerate from 0–60 mph/96 kph in 13.4 seconds. A fuel-injected version, the 190E, was later offered.

Engine	4 cylinder 1997 cc 88 bhp
Length	14 ft 6 in/4.42 m
Width	6 ft/1.83 m
Top speed	107 mph/171 kph
Price new	£10,980
Current	1983–present

MG M Type

The first of the MG Midgets was the M Type of 1929. The little two-seater sports car had much in common with the Morris Minor. Early M Types had fabric-covered bodies. The car's low price helped make sports car ownership more easily affordable, as did a low petrol consumption of 40 mpg. A team of specially tuned Midgets won the Brooklands double-twelve team prize in 1930.

Engine	4 cylinder 847 cc 27 bhp
Length	9 ft 2^1/$_4$ in/2.80 m
Width	4 ft 2 in/1.27 m
Top speed	65 mph/104 kph
Price new	£185
Current	1929–32

MG PA

The MG PA had a chassis based on the earlier J2, and a strengthened engine with a three main bearing crankshaft. MG offered a pretty Airline coupé body on the P Type in addition to the usual open tourers. A team of six women and three cars took part in the 1935 Le Mans race.

Engine	4 cylinder 847 cc 36 bhp
Length	10 ft 11 in/3.33 m
Width	4 ft 4¹/₂ in/1.33 m
Top speed	74 mph/118 kph
Price new	£222
Current	1934–35

MG TF

MG's last car in the old prewar shape was the TF. It was given slight restyling touches, most notably a fake radiator filler cap and a return to octagonal instruments on the dashboard. The 1500 of 1954 had an engine output boosted to 63 bhp, which added to its popularity at the time. The TF series is now a highly sought-after model.

Engine	4 cylinder 1466 cc 63 bhp
Length	12 ft 3 in/3.73 m
Width	5 ft/1.52 m
Top speed	85 mph/136 kph
Price new	£550
Current	1954–55

MGA 1600 Mk II

MG offered a totally redesigned car in the MGA of 1955. The new MG had a sleek aerodynamic shape that was to see few changes during its seven-year production run. The Series II MGA is recognized by its distinctive recessed grille. A twin-cam MGA was produced for two years, but the engine unit proved difficult to maintain and the model was dropped.

Engine	4 cylinder 1622 cc 86 bhp
Length	13 ft/3.96 m
Width	4 ft 10 in/1.47 m
Top speed	97 mph/155 kph
Price new	£963
Current	1961–62

MGB

The MGB replaced the MGA in 1962, and was to sell over half a million units. In later years the chrome bumpers were replaced with rubber ones, largely to meet American safety requirements. In 1980 MG produced a limited edition run of 1000 cars, finished in pewter or bronze metallic paint with a stripe.

Engine	4 cylinder 1798 cc 95 bhp
Length	12 ft 9 in/3.89 m
Width	5 ft/1.52 m
Top speed	107 mph/171 kph
Price new	£5639
Current	1962–80

Mini Cooper S

John Cooper modified the popular Mini to produce the sporting Mini Cooper. The Cooper and Cooper S proved to be brilliant rally cars. A Mini Cooper S driven by Paddy Hopkirk won the 1964 Monte Carlo Rally. The largest engine to be fitted to the range was a 1275 cc unit, which in road-going form gave a 0–60 mph/96 kph acceleration time of 11.2 seconds.

Engine	4 cylinder 1275 cc 76 bhp
Length	10 ft 0¼ in/3.05 m
Width	4 ft 7½ in/1.41 m
Top speed	96 mph/154 kph
Price new	£755
Current	1961–71

Mini Metro

Austin Rover entered the super-mini market with the launch of the Mini Metro. A roomy small car, the Metro has a double folding rear seat, providing extra luggage space. A variety of engine sizes have always been produced. These range from a 998 cc in the basic model to the high performance Metro 16-valve GTi of the 1990s.

Engine	4 cylinder 998 cc 40 bhp
Length	11 ft 2 in/3.40 m
Width	5 ft 1 in/1. 55 m
Top speed	84 mph/134 kph
Price new	£3380
Current	1981–present

Morgan Three-Wheeler

Morgan began by producing three-wheeled cars. The sports three-wheeler was fitted with a lively JAP engine and two-speed gearbox. Morgans were highly placed in trials competitions throughout Britain and Europe. The Aero Sports was replaced by the Super Sports in 1931; this model was intended to rival new cheap sports cars like the MG M Type.

Engine	2 cylinder 1096 cc 10 HP
Length	10 ft 3 in/3.12 m
Width	4 ft 11 in/1.50 m
Top speed	70 mph/112 kph
Price new	£95
Current	1921–30

Morgan 4/44

The Morgan Motor Company is still owned by members of the Morgan Family, making it the oldest family firm in the motor industry. The 4/44 is their longest surviving model. All Morgan cars are still handbuilt, which can lead to a six-year waiting list. The 1982 4/44 had a Ford XR3 engine, which gave a 0–60 mph time of 9 seconds.

Engine	4 cylinder 1597 cc 96 bhp
Length	12 ft/3.66 m
Width	4 ft 8 in/1.42 m
Top speed	103 mph/165 kph
Price new	£7244
Current	1936–present

Morris Bullnose

William Morris began production of his first car, the Morris Oxford, in 1913. The cars were called Bullnose because of their rounded radiators. The Cowley was introduced a little later and the Oxford became the de luxe model. Both models were fitted with Hotchkiss engines after 1920. 10–30 mph/16-48 kph top-gear acceleration took 20 seconds.

Engine	4 cylinder 1805 cc 34 bhp
Length	13 ft 3 in/4.04 m
Width	5 ft/1.52 m
Top speed	55 mph/88 kph
Price new	£260
Current	1913–26

Morris Minor

For years British motor manufacturers tried to develop a car that sold at the magic price of £100. Morris was the first to do so, with the Minor of 1931. The car was a two-seater with no bumpers or chrome. With four-wheel brakes and a petrol consumption of 50 mpg, the Morris Minor was a close rival to the Austin Seven.

Engine	4 cylinder 847 cc 8 HP
Length	9 ft 8 in/2.95 m
Width	4 ft 1½ in/1.26 m
Top speed	56 mph/90 kph
Price new	£100
Current	1931–33

Morris Eight

One of the most popular cars of the 1930s was the Morris Eight. This model helped Morris survive the depression when sales of its other models slumped. The Eight could be purchased as a two- or four-seater saloon, or tourer. A two-tone colour scheme was one of the paint options. Over 350,000 units were sold before the introduction of the Eight Series E.

Engine	4 cylinder 918 cc 29.6 bhp
Length	11 ft 10 in/3.61 m
Width	4 ft 6½ in/1.38 m
Top speed	60 mph/96 kph
Price new	£149
Current	1935–38

Morris Minor

The legendary Morris Minor was designed by Alec Issigonis and was very nearly called the Mosquito. It made its debut at the 1948 London Motor Show where it caused a sensation. The handling set a new standard for small family saloons. Early examples have a split windscreen and headlamps low down into the wings. 0–50 mph/80 kph took 24 seconds.

Engine	4 cylinder 919 cc 27 bhp
Length	12 ft 4 in/3.76 m
Width	5 ft 1 in/1.55 m
Top speed	62 mph/99 kph
Price new	£359
Current	1949–71

Napier Gordon Bennett

Napier was the first British car-maker to build cars especially for motor racing. In 1903 the Gordon Bennett Race was held in Southern Ireland and Napier entered three cars. The one illustrated was driven by Charles Jarrott who crashed. After a rebuild, the car was fastest in the next year's eliminating trials. Napiers were painted green. This became Britain's official racing colour.

Engine	4 cylinder 7708 cc
Length	11 ft 5½ in/3.49 m
Width	5 ft 4 in/1.63 m
Top speed	75 mph/120 kph
Price new	N/A
Current	1903–04

Nash-Healey Convertible

Donald Healey and American Company Nash combined to produce the Nash-Healey, a powerful two-seater with a Healey Silverstone chassis and a 3.8 Nash Ambassador engine. Engine capacity was increased to 4138 cc in 1952, when the body was restyled by Pininfarina. Performance was good, with a 0–60 mph/96 kph time of 11.5 seconds. Unfortunately, few units were sold and production ceased in 1954.

Engine	6 cylinder 4138 cc 135 bhp
Length	14 ft/4.27 m
Width	5 ft 3 in/1.60 m
Top speed	108 mph/173 kph
Price new	$5000
Current	1950–54

Nash Metropolitan

The Nash Metropolitan was built by Austin of Great Britain for the Nash Car Company of America. It was intended solely for the American market. The engine was an Austin A40 unit, while the body was an unusual design styled on American lines. A larger 1500 cc engine was fitted for 1955. The 1200 cc engine was able to accelerate to 60 mph/96 kph in 12.3 seconds.

Engine	4 cylinder 1200 cc 42 bhp
Length	12 ft 5 in/3.78 m
Width	5 ft 1½ in/1.56 m
Top speed	73 mph/117 kph
Price new	$1445
Current	1954–61

NSU Ro80

NSU was well known for its small cars, the 1000 and the Prinz. The Ro80 featured advanced design and striking good looks. NSU produced the car for the touring market. Early cars experienced problems with their rotary engines, so NSU fitted a revised Mk II engine with a warning buzzer that sounded if the engine was revved past 6000 rpm.

Engine	2 rotor 1990 cc 115 bhp
Length	15 ft 10 in/4.83 m
Width	5 ft 9½ in/1.77 m
Top speed	110 mph/176 kph
Price new	£3596
Current	1967–77

Opel GT

Opel moved away from its GM family car image to produce the GT in 1969. Although 1100 cc and 1900 cc engines were fitted, the 1900 was the only version offered for export. The GT bodies were built in France and had a sleek aerodynamic shape with unusual concealed headlamps which revolved into use. 0–60 mph/96 kph took 12 seconds.

Engine	4 cylinder 1897 cc 90 bhp
Length	13 ft 6 in/4.11 m
Width	5 ft 2 in/1.57 m
Top speed	115 mph/184 kph
Price new	£1967
Current	1969–73

Opel Manta

Opel designed its first Manta in 1970, designed to compete in the BMW market. GM produced a re-styled Opel Manta Coupé in 1982, and the next year saw the introduction of a larger fuel-injected engine, which gave a much better performance. The 2 litre unit was the same as that fitted in the Vauxhall Carlton. 0–60 mph/96 kph took 8.5 seconds.

Engine	4 cylinder 1979 cc 110 bhp
Length	14 ft 8 in/4.47 m
Width	5 ft 6 in/1.68 m
Top speed	120 mph/192 kph
Price new	£6445
Current	1982–88

Packard 645

Packard dominated the American luxury car market in the 1920s and 1930s. In 1929 the six series was only built with eight-cylinder engines. Many Packards had coach-built bodies; the 645 had a choice of 13 body styles from coach-builders Le Baron, Rollston and Dietrich (illustrated here). Packard's advertising slogan was 'Ask the man who owns one'.

Engine	8 cylinder 6306 cc 90 bhp
Length	17 ft 10 in/5.44 m
Width	6 ft/1.83 m
Top speed	75 mph/120 kph
Price new	$5985
Current	1929

Packard V12

Packard continued to build big luxury cars during the 1930s. In 1935 it entered the smaller, lower-priced market with the 120 series. At the other end of the scale was the V12, which had a smooth-running engine of 7.5 litres capacity and was available in a variety of body styles.

Engine	V12 7757 cc 175 bhp
Length	17 ft 1½ in/5.22 m
Width	6 ft 2 in/1.88 m
Top speed	92 mph/147 kph
Price new	£1895
Current	1936–39

Pegaso Z102B

Pegaso was one of the few Spanish marques in existence after World War II, and even so only produced a limited number of cars. The first cars were built at the old Hispano-Suiza factory in Barcelona. Designed by Wilfred Ricart, Pegaso offered a choice of V8, 2.5 or 2.8 litre engines. Touring of Milan built some of the most popular body styles in aluminium.

Engine	8 cylinder 2816 cc 170 bhp
Length	13 ft 6 in/4.11 m
Width	5 ft 3 in/1.60 m
Top speed	120 mph/192 kph
Price new	£1600
Current	1951–58

Peugeot 302

Peugeot began to produce cars with a more streamlined appearance with the introduction of its 02 series. The headlamps and the two batteries were placed between the radiator and radiator grille. Models in this range were the 202, 302 and 402. There was also an option known as the 402L, in which a 402 engine was fitted in the smaller 302 car.

Engine	4 cylinder 1758 cc 43 bhp
Length	13 ft 6 in/4.11 m
Width	4 10³/₄ in/1.49 m
Top speed	62 mph/99 kph
Price new	£260
Current	1936–39

Peugeot 504i Cabriolet

Pininfarina created the stylish good looks of the Peugeot 504 series. This was one of the largest models in a range that started with the small 104 and finished with the V6-engined 604. Fuel injection was fitted for the first time in 1969. Acceleration from 0–60 mph/96 kph took 12.4 seconds. The range also included cabriolet versions of the 304 and 504 models.

Engine	4 cylinder 1971 cc 97 bhp
Length	14 ft 2 in/4.32 m
Width	5 ft 6½ in/1.69 m
Top speed	103 mph/165 kph
Price new	£3158
Current	1968–82

Peugeot 205 GTi

Peugeot's 205 GTi emerged as the leader of the 'hot' hatchbacks soon after its introduction in 1984. Fast and affordable, the Peugeot also possessed outstanding roadholding. The model proved to be so popular that a cabriolet version was made available for 1986, the same year that the 1.9 GTi was produced. Acceleration from 0–60 mph/96 kph took 7.1 seconds, and 0–100 mph/160 kph 22 seconds.

Engine	4 cylinder 1905 cc 130 bhp
Length	12 ft 2 in/3.71 m
Width	5 ft 1½ in/1.56 m
Top speed	123 mph/197 kph
Price new	£9295
Current	1984–95

Pierce-Arrow Model 53

Pierce-Arrow was a maker of luxurious American cars which ceased production in 1938. Its cars carried a kneeling archer mascot on the radiator during the 1930s. Two sizes of model 53 were offered on a 137 in or 142 in wheelbase, with an engine cubic displacement of 398 and 429 cu. in. The smaller V12 engine was not particularly powerful but very smooth.

Engine	12 cylinder 6500 cc 140 bhp
Length	16 ft 10½ in/5.14 m
Width	6 ft 1½ in/1.87 m
Top speed	90 mph/144 kph
Price new	$3295
Current	1931–32

Plymouth Superbird

Plymouth built over 1900 Superbirds so that the company could enter the cars for NASCAR racing. Superbirds were based on the Roadrunner series that came complete with Warner Brothers Roadrunner decals at the rear of the car. Standard road-going cars had a 440 cu. in. Magnum engine, while the competition model had a 426 cu. in. hemi-headed unit and a top speed of over 220 mph/352 kph.

Engine	V8 7207 cc 375 bhp
Length	16 ft 10½ in/5.14 m
Width	6 ft 6 in/1.98 m
Top speed	130 mph/208 kph
Price new	N/A
Current	1970

Pontiac GTO

Car enthusiasts were horrified when Pontiac used the same designation as the Ferrari GTO. However, like its namesake, the Pontiac GTO also turned out to be a capable high-performance car. In standard form the 6.5 litre engine was fitted with a single four-barrel carburettor and twin exhausts. This produced a 0–60 mph/96 kph acceleration time of 5.7 seconds.

Engine	V8 6377 cc 325 bhp
Length	16 ft 11 in/5.16 m
Width	6 ft 1 in/1.85 m
Top speed	122 mph/195 kph
Price new	£3420
Current	1964–71

Pontiac Trans Am Firebird

Following on from the success of the GTO, Pontiac produced the Trans Am, designed to compete in America's 'Pony Car' market alongside rivals like the Ford Mustang. The model still remains in production, although some of its early performance has been curtailed by American exhaust emission controls. The 1980 V8 Trans Am Firebird had a 0–60 mph/96 kph acceleration time of 9.4 seconds.

Engine	V8 6500 cc 180 bhp
Length	16 ft 5 in/5 m
Width	6 ft 1¼ in/1.86 m
Top speed	120 mph/192 kph
Price new	$7480
Current	1969–present

Porsche 356

The first car produced in Dr Ferdinand Porsche's own name was the Type 356. It was related to the Volkswagen Beetle and shared an air-cooled rear engine design. Early models also shared a Volkswagen gearbox. The Type 356 was expensive when exported abroad, but was much admired for its aerodynamic shape, roadholding and effortless 70 mph/112 kph cruising speed.

Engine	4 cylinder 1286 cc 44 bhp
Length	12 ft 7$\frac{1}{2}$ in/3.85 m
Width	5 ft 5$\frac{1}{4}$ in/1.66 m
Top speed	85 mph/136 kph
Price new	£1971
Current	1949–65

Porsche 911 Carrera

Based on the long-running 911 series, the Carrera was virtually identical in shape to the 911, except for the large duck-tail spoiler at the rear, and front air dam. The six-cylinder engine had a magnesium crankcase, which was of a hard-wearing design. 0–60 mph/96 kph acceleration took 5.5 seconds. Engine cubic capacity increased over the years from 2.0 to 3.3 litres.

Engine	6 cylinder 2687 cc 210 bhp
Length	14 ft 1 in/4.29 m
Width	5 ft 3 in/1.60 m
Top speed	150 mph/240 kph
Price new	£9000
Current	1965–present

Porsche 968

Porsche updated its 944 series for 1992 and renamed it the 968. Features of the new model include a six-speed gearbox and variable camshaft system. A four-speed Tiptronic semi-automatic gearbox is an optional feature. The company intended the 968 to be one of the most affordably priced Porsches available. Acceleration from 0–60 mph/96 kph takes 6.1 seconds.

Engine	6 cylinder 2990 cc 240 bhp
Length	14 ft 2 in/4.32 m
Width	5 ft 8¼ in/1.73 m
Top speed	153 mph/245 kph
Price new	£34,945
Current	1992–present

Railton Straight Eight

Noel Macklin and some of the old Invicta team produced the Railton in 1933. Designed by Reid Railton as a sporting car based on the American Hudson Terraplane, the Railton offered fine acceleration and performance at a good price. The Straight Eight model was produced in the largest numbers. Hydraulic brakes were fitted in 1936. 0–60 mph/96 kph acceleration took 11.5 seconds.

Engine	8 cylinder 4168 cc 112 bhp
Length	14 ft 5 in/4.39 m
Width	5 ft 8 in/1.73 m
Top speed	91 mph/146 kph
Price new	£628
Current	1933–39

Range Rover

1970 saw the introduction of the Range Rover. Although designed to be just as competent off-road as the Land Rover, it was more comfortable and consequently expensive. Always very popular, latter-day Range Rovers are as luxurious as executive-style saloons. Optional extras include cruise control and air conditioning. An all-alloy V8 engine powers the car from 0–60 mph/96 kph in 10.8 seconds.

Engine	V8 3947 cc 178 bhp
Length	14 ft 8 in/4.47 m
Width	5 ft 10 in/1.78 m
Top speed	107 mph/171 kph
Price new	£35,910
Current	1970–present

Reliant Scimitar

The Reliant Scimitar was one of the first sporting estate cars.
The bodywork was made of fibreglass based on a steel chassis. HRH Princess Anne was a great fan of the Scimitar and
owned at least seven. A convertible version, the GTC, was
offered in 1980. Scimitars were powered by a Ford V6 engine
and could accelerate from 0–60 mph/96 kph in 10.8 seconds.

Engine	6 cylinder 2792 cc 135 bhp
Length	14 ft 2 in/4.32 m
Width	5 ft 6 in/1.68 m
Top speed	116 mph/186 kph
Price new	£11,790
Current	1968–86

Renault 4

Renault produced the 4CV as its answer to Citroën's 2CV. It was to be an all-purpose people's car available at a low price. A rear-opening fifth door made the Renault 4 one of the first hatchbacks. Early 4s had a 747 cc engine which was eventually replaced by one of 845 cc. A four-speed gearbox was fitted in 1967. Acceleration from 0–60 mph/96 kph took 32.1 seconds.

Engine	4 cylinder 845 cc 28 bhp
Length	12 ft 0½ in/3.67 m
Width	4 ft 1½ in/1.26 m
Top speed	72 mph/115 kph
Price new	£1295
Current	1962–86

Renault 5

Renault introduced the 5 in 1972. Over the years the Renault 5 has become one of the world's most popular cars. It received a complete facelift in 1984, becoming slightly larger and roomier with a choice of engine options. The smallest engine, the 956 cc, had a 0–62 mph/99 kph acceleration time of 19.3 seconds. The Renault 5 Turbo took 7.7 seconds.

Engine	4 cylinder 956 cc 42 bhp
Length	11 ft 9½ in/3.59 m
Width	5 ft 2½ in/1.59 m
Top speed	85 mph/136 kph
Price new	£3290
Current	1972–92

Riley 9

Riley Cars kept its reputation for excellent sporting saloons until its merger with Morris in 1938. The Riley 9 of 1936 was redesigned with a new chassis frame and rod brakes. Later 9s had twin carburettors fitted as standard, and a pre-selector gearbox. In acceleration tests, 0–50 mph/80 kph took 36 seconds.

Engine	4 cylinder 1089 cc 42 bhp
Length	13 ft 10 in/4.22 m
Width	4 ft 10 in/1.47 m
Top speed	65 mph/104 kph
Price new	£275
Current	1927–37

Riley RMF 2.5

Last of the traditional Rileys was the RM series. An elegant design, they were also the final Rileys to be designed with running boards. RMs were entered in events such as the Monte Carlo and Daily Express rallies. The 2.5 litre RMF had a very robust engine unit that was occasionally used in boats. 0–60 mph/96 kph acceleration took 16.4 seconds.

Engine	4 cylinder 2443 cc 100 bhp
Length	14 ft 11 in/4.55 m
Width	5 ft 3½ in/1.61 m
Top speed	95 mph/152 kph
Price new	£1642
Current	1952–54

Rolls-Royce Silver Ghost

Unofficially known as the 'Best Car in the World', the Silver Ghost was first shown at the London Motor Show in 1906. Originally the name was given to one particular car that took part in a 15,000 mile reliability run in 1907, but was soon given to all 40–50 HP Rolls-Royce cars. The engine was a straight six L-head with a seven-bearing crankshaft.

Engine	6 cylinder 7046 cc 48 HP
Length	15 ft 6 in/4.72 m
Width	5 ft 7 in/1.70 m
Top speed	65 mph/104 kph
Price new	£985 chassis only
Current	1907–25

Rolls-Royce Alpine Eagle

A sporting version of the Rolls-Royce 40-50 HP was known as the Alpine Eagle. A team of three cars was given several modifications, including a larger radiator and second fuel tank. The team entered the 1913 Austrian Alpine Trial and won six awards and the Archduke Leopold Cup. The model was then marketed as the Alpine.

Engine	6 cylinder 7428 cc 65 bhp
Length	15 ft 7 in/4.75 m
Width	5 ft 10 ¼ in/1.78 m
Top speed	82 mph/131 kph
Price new	£985 chassis only
Current	1913–14

Rolls-Royce Phantom I

Rolls-Royce's long-running 40-50 HP Silver Ghost ceased production in 1925, and was immediately replaced by the Phantom I. Powered by a pushrod-operated overhead-valve engine, the Phantom I was originally known as the 'New Phantom'. Many elegant coach-built bodies were put onto the Phantom I chassis; the car pictured here has one by American coach-builder Brewster.

Engine	6 cylinder 7679 cc 108 bhp
Length	14 ft 10 in/4.52 m
Width	5 ft 10 in/1.78 m
Top speed	75 mph/120 kph
Price new	£1850 chassis only
Current	1925–29

Rolls-Royce Phantom III

Introduced in 1935, the Rolls-Royce Phantom III was a big technical advance for the company. The V12 engine was influenced by Rolls-Royce aero engine designs and was very complex. The Phantom III was also the first Rolls to have independent front suspension. An overdrive gearbox was fitted to later models. A Phantom III could accelerate from 0–60 mph/96 kph in 16.8 seconds.

Engine	12 cylinder 7340 cc
Length	17 ft 9 in/5.41 m
Width	6 ft 3 in/1.91 m
Top speed	100 mph/160 kph
Price new	£1900 chassis only
Current	1935–39

Rolls-Royce Silver Dawn

Originally intended for export only, the first Silver Dawns were fitted with left-hand drive. Later models were produced to include the British market, and were made to appeal to the owner-driver. Based on the Silver Wraith, the Dawn had a shortened wheelbase and an all-steel body manufactured by Rolls-Royce. A typical 0–60 mph/96 kph acceleration time for a Wraith or Silver Dawn was 24 seconds.

Engine	6 cylinder 4566 cc
Length	16 ft 11½ in/5.17 m
Width	5 ft 10 in/1.78 m
Top speed	86 mph/138 kph
Price new	£4605
Current	1949–55

Rolls-Royce Camargue

At the time of its introduction, the Rolls-Royce Camargue was the most expensive model Rolls-Royce had ever produced. Pininfarina designed the two-door bodywork which was based on the Silver Shadow chassis. The Camargue was intended for use as a personal car, and one of its major new features was an automatic air-conditioning system. A General Motors automatic gearbox was fitted as standard.

Engine	V8 6750 cc 218 bhp
Length	17 ft/5.18 m
Width	6 ft 4 in/1.93 m
Top speed	120 mph/192 kph
Price new	£82,122
Current	1975–85

Rover 100 P4

Car buyers of 1960 had a choice in the Rover P4 range, of the four-cylinder 80 or six-cylinder 100. Both models were a continuation of the P4 Rovers introduced in 1949. The cars originally had a centrally mounted headlamp recessed into the grille. This earned the P4 the nickname 'Cyclops'. The 1960 100 engine was a development of the 3 litre unit and was able to reach 50 mph/80 kph in 12 seconds.

Engine	6 cylinder 2625 cc 104 bhp
Length	14 ft 10¼ in/4.53 m
Width	5 ft 5½ in/1.66 m
Top speed	90 mph/144 kph
Price new	£1539
Current	1960–62

Rover 2000

Rover launched an all-new design in 1963 with the introduction of the 2000 P6. The engine was powered by a four-cylinder overhead camshaft unit. Standard P6s had a 0–60 mph/96 kph acceleration time of 15.1 seconds. A twin-carburettored version was produced in 1967, and a high-performance version, the V8, went on sale in October 1971.

Engine	4 cylinder 1978 cc 90 bhp
Length	14 ft 9 in/4.50 m
Width	5 ft 6 in/1.68 m
Top speed	102 mph/163 kph
Price new	£1357
Current	1963–76

Saab 96

Swedish aircraft manufacturers Svenska Aeroplan AB began car production in 1949 with the Saab 92. In common with all early Saabs, the 96 was fitted with a two-stroke engine until 1966 when Saab changed over to Ford V4 engine units. The Saab 96 was a long-lived design that continued with very few alterations until 1980.

Engine	2 cylinder 841 cc 38 bhp
Length	13 ft 8 in/4.17 m
Width	5 ft 2 in/1.57 m
Top speed	72 mph/115 kph
Price new	£729
Current	1960–80

Saab 900 Turbo

Saab introduced a completely different design known as the 99 in 1967. The model proved successful and in 1978 Saab produced the 99 Turbo, one of the first production turbo saloon cars. During this period the 900 series evolved which shared styling similarities with the 99. The 900 was produced with the usual Saab safety features, including wash-wipe headlights and self-repairing bumpers.

Engine	4 cylinder 1985 cc 145 bhp
Length	15 ft 6½ in/4.74 m
Width	5 ft 6½ in/1.69 m
Top speed	112 mph/179 kph
Price new	£11,176
Current	1979–present

Standard Vanguard

Standard's Vanguard of the late 1940s was one of the first new-look postwar cars to be produced. Its appearance was influenced by contemporary American styling. The Vanguard had a three-speed gearbox with steering column gear change, and an umbrella-style handbrake. A tough, reliable family car, the engine unit was used in the Triumph TR series and Ferguson tractor.

Engine	4 cylinder 2088 cc 68 bhp
Length	13 ft 8 in/4.17 m
Width	5 ft 9 in/1.75 m
Top speed	80 mph/128 kph
Price new	£704
Current	1947–63

Stanley Steamer 735

One of the few successful alternatives to the petrol engine was the steam car. A popular make, along with White and Doble, was the Stanley steam car. Steam cars began to lose sales in the 1920s. This was because they took a long time to start from cold. The Stanley 735 of 1920 looked like a petrol car but the radiator was a dummy.

Engine	2 cylinder 16.5 HP
Length	10 ft 10 in/3.30 m
Width	4 ft 8 in/1.42 m
Top speed	65 mph/104 kph
Price new	£1750
Current	1919–22

Studebaker President Roadster

Studebaker offered three series of cars throughout the 1930s. They were the President, Commander and Dictator. Cars in the President series were all fitted with robust eight-cylinder engines and were aimed at the more expensive end of the car-buying market. All were fitted with safety glass, a synchromesh gearbox and optional free-wheel unit.

Engine	8 cylinder 5522 cc 122 bhp
Length	16 ft 2 in/4.93 m
Width	6 ft/1.83 m
Top speed	85 mph/136 kph
Price new	$1950
Current	1929–33

Studebaker DV22

Introduced in 1932, the DV22 was a sports saloon based on the earlier 100 mph Super Bearcat. The engine unit was a twin overhead camshaft straight eight. Stutz exported engines and chassis to Great Britain, where they were bodied by English coach-builders. Although not as fast as the Bearcat, the DV22 could accelerate from 10–30 mph/16-48 kph in 5.5 seconds.

Engine	8 cylinder 5277 cc 156 bhp
Length	16 ft/4.88 m
Width	6 ft/1.83 m
Top speed	90 mph/144 kph
Price new	£1695
Current	1932–35

Studebaker Avanti

When Raymond Loewy created the Studebaker Avanti, it had a remarkably streamlined shape for the period. Built in fibreglass, original features included a built-in rollbar and caliper disc brakes. The Avanti was a fine performer, but Studebaker stopped producing it in 1964. The car returned in 1965 as a marque in its own right known as the Avanti.

Engine	V8 4734 cc 240 bhp
Length	16 ft/4.88 m
Width	5 ft 10 in/1.78 m
Top speed	117 mph/187 kph
Price new	$4445
Current	1963–64

Stutz Roadster

Stutz began life as the Ideal Motor Company but changed its name in 1913. The company's Roadster and Bearcat models were designed to rival the Mercer Raceabout, and a strong following grew around both manufacturers. Body design was a stark two-seater sports, with a round petrol tank placed immediately behind the rear seats. Unusually, the gearbox was integrated with the rear axle.

Engine	4 cylinder 6372 cc 60 bhp
Length	10 ft/3.05 m
Width	4 ft 8 in/1.42 m
Top speed	70 mph/112 kph
Price new	$2000
Current	1913–17

Sunbeam-Talbot 10

Rootes took over the firms of Sunbeam and Talbot in 1935, making the subsequent Sunbeam-Talbot 10 and larger 2 litre model an entirely Rootes design. Mechanically the 10 was based on the Hillman Minx, and had good handling capabilities. Although the 10 was a small car, its interior had a high-quality finish. 0–60 mph/96 kph took 38.7 seconds.

Engine	4 cylinder 1185 cc 41 bhp
Length	12 ft 11½ in/3.95 m
Width	4 ft 11 in/1.50 m
Top speed	66 mph/106 kph
Price new	£685
Current	1938–48

Sunbeam Alpine

Named after the Alpine rally successes enjoyed by Sunbeam, the Sunbeam Alpine was conceived as a two-seater sports car that would sell in the United States. An early works prototype driven by Stirling Moss and Sheila Van Damm covered the flying kilometre at 120.125 mph/192 kph at Jabbeke in Belgium in 1953. Standard Alpines could manage 0–60 mph/96 kph in 11.5 seconds.

Engine	4 cylinder 2267 cc 80 bhp
Length	14 ft 0¼ in/4.27 m
Width	5 ft 2½ in/1.59 m
Top speed	95 mph/152 kph
Price new	£895
Current	1953–54

Talbot 105

Clement-Talbot produced some of its finest cars in the 1930s. The six-cylinder cars were designed by George Roesch, who was a brilliant engineer. Many types of bodywork were offered on the 105 chassis, ranging from a saloon and airline saloon to a sports tourer. A Talbot 105 could cruise at 70 mph/112 kph, and 0–50 mph/80 kph took 15.5 seconds.

Engine	6 cylinder 2970 cc 100 bhp
Length	15 ft 8 in/4.78 m
Width	5 ft 9 in/1.75 m
Top speed	88 mph/141 kph
Price new	£805
Current	1931–37

Talbot Lago Grand Sport

Major Anthony Lago took control of the old Sunbeam-Talbot Darracq works in France, and combined the production of racing cars with that of luxurious Grand Touring cars, bodied by the best coach-builders of the day. Lago resumed postwar car production with the Record and Grand Sport. The powerful overhead-valve engine was fitted with three Stromberg carburettors.

Engine	6 cylinder 4482 cc 190 bhp
Length	N/A
Width	N/A
Top speed	124 mph/198 kph
Price new	N/A
Current	1947–54

Toyota MR2

Toyota was the first Japanese car-maker to offer a mid-engined sports car in the MR2. It was a proper two-seater with unusual wedge-shaped styling. The 1587 cc engine offered powerful performance allied with a touring petrol consumption of 38 mpg. 0–60 mph/96 kph acceleration took 8 seconds. Favourable comments were made about the MR2's handling, despite its engine location.

Engine	4 cylinder 1587 cc 122 bhp
Length	12 ft 10$\frac{1}{2}$ in/3.92 m
Width	5 ft 5$\frac{1}{2}$ in/1.66 m
Top speed	121 mph/194 kph
Price new	£11,990
Current	1985–90

Triumph Dolomite

An unusual waterfall radiator was the most striking feature of Triumph's elegant Dolomite series. Available as roadster or saloon, Dolomites were first of all fitted with a four-cylinder engine. A six-cylinder 2 litre version with three carburettors became available later in 1938. The roadster was essentially a two- or occasional three-seater with a dickey seat at the back.

Engine	4 cylinder 1767 cc 55 bhp
Length	14 ft/4.27 m
Width	5 ft 5 in/1.65 m
Top speed	75 mph/120 kph
Price new	£348
Current	1936–39

Triumph 1800 Roadster

A Triumph Roadster was one of the stars of the British TV detective series *Bergerac*. Roadsters had a 7 in shorter wheelbase than the razor-edge saloon car they were based on. The first Roadsters had 1800 cc engines, but a 2000 cc version took over in 1948. Triumph Roadsters were the last British cars to be designed with a dickey seat at the rear.

Engine	4 cylinder 1776 cc 68 bhp
Length	14 ft 0$^1\!/_2$ in/4.28 m
Width	5 ft 4 in/1.63 m
Top speed	70 mph/112 kph
Price new	£775
Current	1946–48

Triumph Mayflower

The razor-edge style of the Triumph Mayflower, based on the Triumph Renown, was controversial at the time of its launch. At first the motoring press was unkind about its looks, and one reviewer pronounced it 'as streamlined as King Farouk'. In spite of this, the Mayflower had good visibility, was roomy and easy to handle. 0–60 mph/96 kph acceleration took 42.6 seconds.

Engine	4 cylinder 1247 cc 38 bhp
Length	13 ft/3.96 m
Width	5 ft 2 in/1.57 m
Top speed	63 mph/101 kph
Price new	£450
Current	1949–53

Triumph TR2

The early 1950s saw the successful development and export of sports cars such as the MG TD and Jaguar XK120. Triumph very quickly designed the TR2 as competition. Powered by a modified Standard Vanguard engine, the TR2 enjoyed great success in the export market, particularly to the USA. 0–60 mph/96 kph acceleration took 11.9 seconds.

Engine	4 cylinder 1991 cc 90 bhp
Length	12 ft 7 in/3.84 m
Width	4 ft 7½ in/1.41 m
Top speed	107 mph/171 kph
Price new	£865
Current	1953–55

Triumph TR4

Michelotti designed the all-new shape of the Triumph TR4 of 1961. Much of the chassis was still based on the old TR3 series. Optional extras on the TR4 were overdrive and an ingenious two-piece hardtop. A few TR4s were used in events such as the Alpine Rally. Acceleration from 0–60 mph/96 kph took 10.9 seconds.

Engine	4 cylinder 2138 cc 100 bhp
Length	13 ft/3.96 m
Width	4 ft 10 in/1.47 m
Top speed	102 mph/163 kph
Price new	£907
Current	1961–65

Triumph Herald

The Herald caused a sensation when launched in 1959. It was a family car with independent rear suspension and Italian styling by Michelotti. Most surprising was the Herald's turning circle. One motoring writer noted that it was possible to park the car with only 18 in/45 cm clearance front and rear. The whole of the front tilted forward for easy access.

Engine	4 cylinder 848 cc 34.5 bhp
Length	12 ft 9 in/3.89 m
Width	5 ft/1.52 m
Top speed	70 mph/112 kph
Price new	£702
Current	1959–71

Triumph Stag

A rival to Porsche, Alfa Romeo and Mercedes was how Triumph saw the Stag of 1970. The twin carburettored V8 engine unit was a close relation to that fitted to the Saab 99. Power steering was fitted as standard, overdrive was an optional extra. Fuel consumption for the size of engine was good at 22 mpg. 0–60 mph/96 kph took 9.7 seconds.

Engine	V8 2997 cc 145 bhp
Length	14 ft 6½ in/4.43 m
Width	5 ft 3½ in/1.61 m
Top speed	115 mph/184 kph
Price new	£2094
Current	1970–77

Trojan PB

The Trojan was one of the last cars to be fitted with solid tyres. The wheels were narrow enough to fall into tramlines – a fate to be avoided as the car could end up travelling to the tram depot. The reliable engine was housed under the floorboards, and contained only seven moving parts.

Engine	4 cylinder 1523 cc 20 bhp
Length	8 ft/2.44 m
Width	4 ft/1.22 m
Top speed	35 mph/56 kph
Price new	£157
Current	1923–25

Tucker Torpedo

Preston Tucker was a showman-like figure and the subject of a Francis Ford Coppola film in 1988. The Tucker Torpedo was a streamlined full six-seater with several unusual features, including a central headlamp that turned with the wheels. Powered by an Air Cooled Motors flat-six engine, but converted to water-cooling, the Torpedo could accelerate from 0–60 mph/96 kph in 10 seconds.

Engine	6 cylinder 5487 cc 166 bhp
Length	18 ft 3 in/5.56 m
Width	N/A
Top speed	120 mph/192 kph
Price new	$2245
Current	1947–48

TVR Chimaera

TVR introduced the Chimaera at the 1992 Birmingham Motor Show. It was designed to replace the Griffith which had been phased out in 1991. Rover currently supplies the engine unit, which can be bought in 4.0 or 4.3 litre versions, although tuning is by TVR Power. The bodywork is fibreglass on a multi-tubular chassis. 0–60 mph/96 kph takes 5.2 seconds.

Engine	8 cylinder 3950 cc 240 bhp
Length	12 ft 9^1/$_4$ in/3.89 m
Width	6 ft 4^1/$_2$ in/1.94 m
Top speed	158 mph/253 kph
Price new	£26,250
Current	1993–present

Vanden Plas 1300

In 1946 Austin took over the British arm of the Belgian coach-builders Vanden Plas, and from 1960 the company produced cars in its own right. The Vanden Plas 1300 was based on the bestselling BMC 1100/1300 series, designed by Alec Issigonis. The cars were trimmed to a high standard and fittings included leather seats, wooden veneer, picnic tables and an optional sunroof.

Engine	4 cylinder 1275 cc 65 bhp
Length	12 ft 3¼ in/3.74 m
Width	5 ft 0½ in/1.54 m
Top speed	91 mph/146 kph
Price new	£1650
Current	1967–74

Vauxhall Prince Henry

Designed by Lawrence Pomeroy, the Vauxhall Prince Henry was one of the first true sports cars. The 4 litre models of 1913 were descended from a team of 3 litre cars entered in the German Prince Henry trials. Vauxhall won and so its sporting car series was named in honour of the event.

Engine	4 cylinder 3969 cc 70 bhp
Length	13 ft 11 in/4.24 m
Width	5 ft 8 in/1.73 m
Top speed	75 mph/120 kph
Price new	£615
Current	1913–15

Vauxhall Calibra

Vauxhall moved away from its family saloon car image to produce the Calibra in 1990. Although able to seat four people, styling is that of a sports coupé. *Autocar* and *Motor* awarded the Calibra the Best Design award of 1989. Four-wheel drive was made available from November 1990. The 16-valve 2 litre engine accelerates from 0–60 mph/96 kph in 8.1 seconds.

Engine	4 cylinder 1998 cc 150 bhp
Length	14 ft 9 in/4.50 m
Width	5 ft 6½ in/1.69 m
Top speed	137 mph/219 kph
Price new	£18,550
Current	1990–present

Vauxhall Lotus Carlton

Vauxhall joined forces with high-performance specialists Lotus to produce the world's fastest production family saloon in the Vauxhall Lotus Carlton. As a high-speed road car it was also one of the safest. With powerful anti-lock brakes and a six-speed gearbox, the Vauxhall Carlton chassis was a good match for the twin turbo-charged Lotus engine. 0–60 mph/96 kph took 5.1 seconds.

Engine	6 cylinder 3615 cc 377 bhp
Length	15 ft 7¾ in/4.77 m
Width	6 ft 4 in/1.93 m
Top speed	165 mph/264 kph
Price new	£49,043
Current	1990–94

Volkswagen Beetle

Ferdinand Porsche began to design Adolf Hitler's 'people's car' in 1934. Hitler specified that it should be a car that everyone could afford. There was even a scheme to buy it using saving stamps. Postwar production started in 1947. It is still produced in some countries and is now the world's bestselling car ever, with sales of over 20 million.

Engine	4 cylinder 1131 cc 24.5 bhp
Length	13 ft 4¼ in/4.07 m
Width	5 ft 0¼ in/1.53 m
Top speed	63 mph/101 kph
Price new	£690
Current	1947–present

Volkswagen Golf GTi

Volkswagen produced the first of the 'hot' hatchbacks, the GTi, in 1976. Right-hand drive models went on sale in 1979. The GTi was fitted with Bosch K-Jetronic fuel injection, and a five-speed gearbox was standard from 1981. Volkswagen's nearest rivals to the GTi were the Alfasud and Ford Escort XR3. 0–60 mph/96 kph took 9 seconds.

Engine	4 cylinder 1588 cc 110 bhp
Length	12 ft 6¼ in/3.82 m
Width	5 ft 4 in/1.63 m
Top speed	111 mph/178 kph
Price new	£5700
Current	1976–present

Volkswagen Corrado

Volkswagen's performance car, the Corrado, shared a 2 litre engine with the Passat. A later 190 bhp version used the VR6 power unit. Road-testers praised the Corrado's front-wheel drive chassis. A unique styling feature was the moving rear spoiler, which raised automatically when the car reached 45 mph/72 kph. Acceleration from 0–60 mph/96 kph took 6.4 seconds.

Engine	4 cylinder 1984 cc 190 bhp
Length	13 ft 3^1/$_2$ in/4.05 m
Width	5 ft 6 in/1.68 m
Top speed	126 mph/202 kph
Price new	£21,999
Current	1989–95

Volvo 122S

Volvo's early concern for car safety showed in its 121/122 series, which was fitted with seat belts as early as 1962. Known unofficially as the Amazon, the solidly well-built 120 models sold in great numbers abroad. Later, 122S Volvos were fitted with the new 90 bhp B12 engine that helped acceleration. 0–60 mph/96 kph took 16.4 seconds.

Engine	4 cylinder 1780 cc 90 bhp
Length	14 ft 7½ in/4.46 m
Width	4 ft 11½ in/1.51 m
Top speed	99 mph/158 kph
Price new	£1460
Current	1962–70

Volvo PV444

Volvo designed the PV444 during World War II, and the car was exhibited at the 1944 Stockholm Motor Show. Although designed in Sweden, the PV444's looks owed much to American styling influences. Volvo's PV444 was the first Swedish car to be made in large numbers, and to be exported abroad. The average 0–60 mph/96 kph acceleration time was 24.9 seconds.

Engine	4 cylinder 1414 cc 40 bhp
Length	14 ft 4 in/4.37 m
Width	5 ft 2 in/1.58 m
Top speed	74 mph/118 kph
Price new	£448
Current	1944–65

Wolseley Hornet

Wolseley pioneered the use of a small six-cylinder engine in its Hornet of 1930. The first Hornets shared many components with the Morris Minor. The size of its engine made the Hornet a useful base for conversion from saloon to sporting car. Various coach-builders made sports Hornets, and some of the best known were Eustace Watkins, Arrow and Swallow.

Engine	6 cylinder 1261 cc 47 bhp
Length	10 ft 6½ in/3.21 m
Width	4 ft 2¼ in/1.28 m
Top speed	70 mph/112 kph
Price new	£225
Current	1930–36

Wolseley Super Six

Wolseley lost its independence to Morris in 1935. Both companies then became part of BMC in 1952. After the takeover Wolseleys became more luxurious versions of Morris cars and were often used as police cars. A range of Super Six models was produced, including a 25 HP model with bigger 3.5 litre engine. Wolseley cars had a distinctive illuminated maker's badge on the radiator grille.

Engine	6 cylinder 2062 cc 63.5 bhp
Length	15 ft 7 in/4.75 m
Width	5 ft 10 in/1.78 m
Top speed	66 mph/106 kph
Price new	£325
Current	1935–37

Wolseley 1500

Wolseley 1500s shared many components with other BMC cars, and were slower versions of the Riley 1.5 litre. The 1500 was fitted with Morris Minor suspension and steering and the same engine as the Morris Oxford, but with a modified compression ratio. One road tester commented that ladies viewing his road test car liked the combination of exterior and interior colours.

Engine	4 cylinder 1489 cc 50 bhp
Length	12 ft 7³/₄ in/3.85 m
Width	5 ft 1 in/1.55 m
Top speed	77 mph/123 kph
Price new	£775
Current	1957–65

Selective List of Owners Clubs

The AC Owners Club Ltd
SAE to Mr B.C. Clark
60 Hillcrest Road
Camberley
Surrey GU15 1LG

The AEC Society
SAE to Miss L.D. Harris
32 Kingscroft Road
Hucclecote
Glos GL3 3RG

AJS Car Club
Peter Hubbard
The Chestnuts
Chequers Road
Tharston
Norwich NR15 2YA
Tel: 01508 30072

Alfa Romeo Owners Club
SAE to 97 High Street
Linton
Cambs CB1 6JT
Tel: 01223 894300

Alfa Romeo 1900 Register
SAE to Peter Marshall
Mariners
Courtlands Avenue
Esher
Surrey KT10 9HZ

Alfa Romeo 2600/2000 International
All 102/106 series cars
SAE to Roger Monk
Knighton
Church Close
West Runton
Cromer NR27 9QY

Giulietta Register and Enthusiasts Club
All Giulietta and Giulia 750/101s
Gavin McGuire
Chart House
Morrehouse Road
Limpsfield
Surrey RH8 0SR

Allard Owners Club
SAE to Miss P Hulse
1 Dalmeny Avenue
Tufnell Park
London N7 0LD

The Alvis Register
For 1920-32 cars
SAE to Mr J. Willis
The Vinery
Wanbrough Manor
Near Guildford
Surrey GU3 2JR
Tel: 01483 810308

Alvis Owner Club
SAE to Malcolm Davey
1 Forge Cottages
Little Beyham
Lamberhurst
Kent TN3 8BB
Tel: 01892 890043

American Auto Club UK
SAE to Harry Tune
2 Cumbers Cottage
Sandy Lane
Hanmer
Whitchurch
Shropshire SY13 3DL

Pre '50 American Auto Club
For all American vehicles to 1959
SAE to Ian Herbert
17 Great Fox Meadow
Kelvedon Hatch
Brentwood
Essex CM15 0AU

**Motorvatin' USA American
  Car Club**
Trevor Lynn
PO Box 2222
Braintree
Essex CM7 6TW
Tel: 01376 552478

**Armstrong Siddeley Owners
  Club**
SAE to Peter Sheppard
57 Berberry Close
Bournville
Birmingham B30 1TB
Tel: 0121 459 0742

**Association of Old Vehicle
  Clubs in Northern Ireland**
Trevor Mitchell
38 Ballymaconnell Road
Bangor
Co. Down BT20 5PS
Tel: 01247 467886

**Aston Martin Owners Club
  Ltd**
Jim Whyman
AMOC Ltd
1a High Street
Sutton
Near Ely
Cambs CB6 2RB
Tel: 01353 777353

**Club Audi (incorporating
  Classic Audi Register)**
Mrs Kim Feenan
Market Chambers
High Sreet
Toddington
Beds LU5 6BY
Tel: 01525 873002

Austin J40 Car Club
For J40s and Pathfinders
SAE to A. and J. Parker-
    Mowbray
6 Alpine Close
Gloucester GL4 9QZ

Austin A30-A35 Owners Club
SAE to Graham Cole
Ivydene
Allet
Truro
Cornwall TR4 9DW
Tel: 01872 73938

A40 Farine Club
Large SAE to Geoffrey Goode
1 Dyas Road
Hollywood
Near Birmingham B47 5LE

The 1100 Club
For all derivatives of BMC 1100
    and 1130
SAE to PO Box 3326
London N1 1QD

Allegro Club International
SAE to 20 Stoneleigh Crescent
Stoneleigh
Epsom
Surrey KT19 0RP

Landcrab Owners Club
  International
For Austin-Morris 1800/2200
    and Wolseley 18/85 and Six
Bill Fraser
LOCI
PO Box 218
Cardiff CF3 9HZ

Austin 3 Litre Owners Club
SAE to Barry Gilleland
25 Cranbury Road
Eastleigh
Hants SO5 5HB
Tel: 01703 644369

Austin Maxi Club
SAE to Mrs C. Jackson
27 Queen Street
Bardeny
Lincoln LN3 5XF

Wedge Owners Club
For Austin Princess and
    Ambassador
SAE to Linda Llewellyn
19 Moult Avenue
Spondon
Derbyshire DE21 7FW
Tel: 01332 675263

Austin Cambridge/ Westminster Car Club

For A40/A50/A55/A60/A90/ A95/A110 and derivatives
SAE to Mr J. Curtis
4 Russell Close
East Budleigh
Salterton
Devon EX9 7EH

Metropolitan Owners Club
SAE to South Cottage
School Lane
Washington
Pulborough
West Sussex RH20 4AP
Tel:/Fax: 01903 893264

Austin Counties Car Club

For Austins 8 to 16, A40, A70 and A90
SAE to David Thornton
Post Office Cottage
Pettuagh
Stow Market
Suffolk IP14 6DW
Tel: 01473 890353

Austin Atlantic Owners Club
SAE to Chris Norris
124 Holbrook Road
Stratford
London E15 3DZ
Tel: 0181 534 2682

Austin Sheerline Princess Owners Register

For Austins A125-A135
SAE to Peter Williams
4 The Lodge
Western Road
Crediton
Devon EX17 3NH
Tel: 01363 773274

Austin Gipsy Register

For 1958-68 cars
SAE to Mike Gilbert
24 Green Close
Rixon
Sturminster Newton
Dorset DT10 1BJ

750 Motor Club

Largest club for Austin 7s
Mike Peck
Courthouse
St. Winifred's Road
Biggin Hill
Kent
Tel: 01959 575812/Fax: 01959 540094

Pre-War Austin Seven Club Ltd
SAE to Mr J. Tantum
90 Dovedale Avenue
Long Eaton
Nottingham NG10 3HU
Tel: 01602 727626

Austin Seven Owners Club
For all Austin Sevens 1922-39
SAE to T. & N.M. Simpkins
5 Brook Cottages
Riding Lane
Hildenborough
Kent TN11 9LJ

Austin Big 7 Register
SAE to Mr R.E. Taylor
101 Derby Road
Chellaston
Derby DE73 1SB

Austin Ten Drivers Club Ltd
For 10-28 HP Austins 1931-39
SAE to Mrs Patricia East
Brambledene
53 Oxted Green
Milford
Godalming
Surrey GU8 5DD

Vintage Austin Register
For all 1906-39 Austins
SAE to Frank Smith
The Briars
Four Lane Ends
Oakerthorpe
Alfreton
Derbyshire DE55 7LH
Tel: 01773 831646

Austin Healey Club
SAE to Colleen Holmes
Dept PC
4 Saxby Street
Leicester LE2 0ND

Autovia Car Club
Alan Williams
Birchanger
Near Bishops Stortford
Herts CM23 5QH

Bedford Owners Club
SAE to Ron Ruggins
Dept 2
Corona
Leatherhead
Great Bookham
Surrey KT23 4RB
Tel: 01702 345885

Bentley Drivers Club
For cars 1921 to date
SAE to: 16 Chearsley Road
Long Crendon
Aylesbury
Bucks HP18 9AW
Tel: 01844 208233/Fax: 01844
    208923

Berkeley Enthusiasts Club
SAE to M. Rounsville-Smith
41 Gorsewood Road
St Johns
Woking
Surrey GU21 1UZ
Tel: 01483 475330

The Scottish BMC Car Club
SAE to David Atkings
45 Coylton Crescent
Hamilton
Scotland
Tel: 01698 820062

The BMW Car Club (GB) Ltd
PO Box 328
Andover
Hants SP10 1YN
Tel: 01264 337883

**BMW Drivers Club
  International UK**
Bavaria House
32a High Street
Dereham
Norfolk NR19 1DR
Tel: 01362 694459

Bond Owners Club
*For owners and enthusiasts of
  Bond Minicars, 875s, Bugs
  and Equipes*
SAE to Stan Comock
42 Beaufort Avenue
Hodge Hill
Birmingham B34 6AE

The Bug Club
SAE to Mrs V.V. Woolley
4 Knight Street
Pinchback
Spalding
Lincs PE11 3RB

Borgward Drivers Club
*For all enthusiasts of Borgwards,
  Lloyds, Goliaths and Hanas*
Ian Cave
Natley House
Ridgway
Pyrford
Woking
Surrey GU22 8PW

Bristol Owners Club
SAE to John Emery
Vesutor
Marringdean Road
Billingshurst
Sussex RH14 9EH

Buckler Car Register
All Buckler multitube space frames
SAE to Mr S. Hibberd
52 Greenacres
Wollton Hill
Near Newbury
Berks RG15 9TA

Bugatti Owners Club Ltd
SAE to Sue Ward
Prescott Hill
Gotherington
Cheltenham
Glos GL52 4RD

UK Buick Club
SAE to Alf Gascoine
47 Higham Road
Woodford Green IG8 9JN
Tel: 0181 505 7347

Cambridge Oxford Owners Club
For Cambridges A40-A60, Westminsters A90-A110, Farina Oxfords, Wolseleys, Rileys, Magnettes and Vanden Plas
SAE to 32 Reservoir Road
Southgate
London N14 4BG

Classic Corvette Club (UK)
Keith Beschi
Pencroft
Butchers Lane
Preston
Herts
Tel: 01462 45211

Classic Chevy Club UK
Trevor Lynn
PO Box 2222
Braintree
Essex CM7 6TW
Tel: 01376 552478

Avenger Sunbeam Owners Club
For Hillman Avenger and Chrysler/Talbot Sunbeam (especially Tiger and Lotus models)
ASOC
145 Kingsway
Middleton M24 1HP

Chrysler Corporation Club UK
For pre-1970 Chrylsers, DeSotos, Imperials and Plymouths
Pete Grist
30 Purbrook Close
Lordswood
Southampton SO16 5NZ
Tel: 01703 328032

Australian Chrysler Owners Club
For all models imported 1965-74
SAE to 1 Swan Mead
Luton
Beds LU4 0YP

Citroën Car Club
SAE to Dept Prc
PO Box 348
Bromley
Kent BR2 8QT

2CV GB (Deux Chevaux Club of GB)
PO Box 602
Crick
Northampton NN6 7UW

2CV and Dyane Auto Club of London
PO Box 41
London SE21 8QT

(Citroën) Traction Owners Club
For pre-1957 Citroën cars
SAE to Steve Reed
1 Terwick Cottage
Rogate
Near Petersfield
Hants GU31 5EG

The Citroën Traction Enthusiasts Club
For Citroen Traction Avants 1934-57
SAE to Robin Rother
Preston House Studio
Preston
Canterbury
Kent CT3 1DZ

Clan Crusader Owners Club
SAE to Chris Clay
48 Valley Road
Littleover
Derby DE3 6HS
Tel: 01332 767410

Classic and Historic Motor Club
For all pre-1959 cars
SAE to Francis Baker
451 Locking Road
Weston-super-Mare BS22 8QN

Classic Motor Sports Club
SAE to Stephanie Taylor
37d Heathfield Road
Wandsworth Common
London SW18 2PH

Clyno Register
SAE to Mr R. Surman
Swallow Cottage
Langton Farm
Burbage Common Road
Elmesthorpe
Leics LE9 7SE
Tel: 01455 842178

The Convertible Club
*For all makes and ages of open-top
vehicles*
SAE to PO Box 561
Chippenham
Wilts SN15 1SU

Cougar Club of America
For 1967-73 Mercury Cougars
SAE to Barrie S. Dixon
11 Dean Close
Partington
Manchester M31 4BQ
Tel: 0161 775 0820

**The Crayford Convertible Car
Club**
For cars converted by Crayford
SAE to Rory Cronin
68 Manor Road
Worthing
West Sussex
BN11 4SL

Crossley Climax Register
*For all Crossley Models 1931-37
with Coventry Climax engines*
SAE to Mr M. Sims
10 Longbridge Road
Bramley
Hants RG26 5AN

Crossley Register
*For veteran, vintage and post-
vintage Crossley-engined cars*
Malcolm Jenner
Willow Cottage
Lexham Road
Great Dunham
Kings Lynn
Tel: 01328 701240

DAF Owners Club
SAE to S.K. Bidwell
56 Ridgedale Road
Bolsover
Chesterfield
Derbyshire

**The Daimler and Lanchester
Owners Club**
Also for certain BSAs
John Ridley
Freepost
The Manor House
Trewyn
Abergavenny
Gwent NP7 5BR
Tel: 01873 890737 (office hours)

Datsun Owners Club
*For 120Y,160J, 180B, 240K GT,
    280C, etc.*
3 Dorset Gardens
East Grinstead
West Sussex RH19 2SD
Tel: 01342 324069

Datsun Z Club
*For the Fairlady range, 240Z,
    260Z, 280Z, 280ZX and
    300ZX*
Mark or Margaret Bukowska
Tel: 0181 998 9616

The Classic Z Register
For Datsun 240 and 260Z
Jon and Beverly Newlyn
11 Lawday Link
Upper Hale
Farnham
Surrey GU9 0BS
Tel: 01252 714656

Delahaye Club (GB)
A.F. Harrison
34 Marine Parade
Hythe
Kent CT21 6AN

Dellow Register
SAE c/o Douglas Temple
    Design Group
4 Roumelia Lane
Bournemouth BH5 1ET
Tel: 01202 304641/Fax: 01202
    392170

De Tomaso Drivers Club
Chris Statham
2-4 Bank Road
Bredbury
Stockport
Cheshire SK6 1DR
Tel: 0161 430 5052

The Diva Register
Steve Pethybridge
8 Wait End Road
Waterlooville
Hants PO7 7DD
Tel: 01705 251485

Dutton Owners Club
Amber Upton
2 Rynal Street
Evesham
Worcs WR11 4QA

Elva Owners Club
*For enthusiasts of the Courier and
    the various sports/racing cars*
8 Liverpool Terrace
Worthing
West Sussex BN11 1TA
Tel:/Fax: 01903 823710

Facel Vega Owners Club
Roy Scandrett
Windrush
16 Paddock Gardens
East Grinstead
Sussex RH19 4AE

**Fairthorpe Sports Car Club
(Turner, Rochdale, Tornado,
Ashley, Falcon, E.B. and
Historic Specials Register)**
SAE to Tony Hill
9 Lynhurst Crescent
Hillingdon
Middx UB10 9EF

Ferrari Owners Club
SAE to Peter Everingham
35 Market Place
Snettisham
Kings Lynn
Norfolk PE31 7LR
Tel: 01485 544500

Ferrari Club of GB
Betty Mathias
7 Swan Close
Blakedown
Worcs DY10 3JT
Tel: 01562 700009

Fiat 500 Club
SAE to Mrs J. Westcott
33 Lionel Avenue
Wendover
Bucks HP22 6LP
Tel: 01296 622880

Fiat 130 Owners Club
*For 130 saloons/Farina and
coupés*
SAE to Michael Reid
28 Warwick Mansions
Cromwell Crescent
London SW5 9QR
Tel: 0171 373 9740

Fiat Dino Register
59 Sandown Park
Turnbridge Wells
Kent TN2 4RY

Fiat Motor Club (GB)
H.A. Collyer
Barnside
Chickwell Street
Glastonbury
Somerset BA6 8DB
Tel: 01458 831443

Fiat Osca Register
Mr M. Elliott
36 Maypole Drive
Chigwell
Essex

Fiat Twin-Cam Register
*For 124 Spider and Coupé,
    Abarth Spider, 131 Mirafiori
    and all T/C Fiats*
Graham Morrish
19 Oakley Wood Road
Bishops Tachbrook
Leamington Spa
Warks

X/19 Owners Club
For Bertone/Fiat X/19s
SAE to Steve Cant and Julie
    Fey
25 Windmill Close
Ryde
IOW PO33 3JB
Tel: 01983 562055

Pre-67 Ford Owners Club
Mrs A. Miller
100 Main Street
Cairneyhill
Fife
Tel: 01383 880136

**Ford Anglia 105E Owners
    Club**
*For Anglias (1959-67), including
    123E, 307E/309E and Prefects
    107E*
SAE to Martin Lewis
81 Compton Road
North End
Portsmouth
Hants PO2 0SR

Capri Club Scotland
SAE to Paul McCartney
84 Locksley Avenue
Knightswood
Glasgow
Tel: 0141 954 8319

Capri Club (International)
Field House
Redditch
Worcs B98 0AN
Tel: 01527 502066

**Ford Capri Enthusiasts
    Register**
Michael Webster
34 Warrington Road
Ashton-in-Makerfield
Wigan
Lancs WN4 9PJ

**Ford Capri Drivers
    Association**
SAE to Mrs M. Farrelly
9 Lyndhurst Road
Coulsdon
Surrey CR5 3HU

Southern Capri Club
National Membership
SAE to 857 Great Cambridge
    Road
Enfield
Middlesex EN1 4BX
Tel: 0181 367 0310

The Capri Collection
SAE to PO Box147
Coventry CV6 6DQ

**Ford Classic and Capri
Owners Club**
SAE to Eric Cox
46 South Road
Puckeridge
Near Ware
Herts SG11 1TH

Ford Corsair Owners Club
SAE to Mrs E. Checkley
7 Barnfield
New Malden
Surrey KT3 5RH

**Mk I Consul Zephyr and
Zodiac Owners Club**
180 Gipsy Road
Welling
Kent DA161JQ

**Consul, Zephyr and Zodiac
Mk II Owners Club**
SAE to Ben Haligan
72 Fairway North
Bromborough
Wirral L62 3NA

**Ford Mk II Independent
Owners Club**
*For 1956-62 Consul, Zephyr and
Zodiac cars*
713 Sparrow Farm Drive
Feltham
Middx TW14 0DG
Tel: 0181 384 3559

**Ford Mk III Zephyr and
Zodiac Owners Club**
SAE to 42 Berkeley Road
Hillingdon
Middx UB10 9DX

**The Zephyr and Zodiac Mk
IV Owners Club**
SAE to John Glaysher
94 Claremount Road
Rugby CV21 3 LU

Mk I Cortina Owners Club
SAE to R.J. Raisey
51 Studley Rise
Trowbridge
Wilts BA14 0PD
Tel: 01225 763888

Cortina Mk II Owners Club
For all models, including 1600E,
*   GT Lotus and Savage*
SAE to 78 Church Avenue
Broomfield
Chelmsford
Essex CM1 5HA

Ford Cortina Mk III Owners
**   Club**
Maurice Hunter
61 Cardigan Road
Bedworth
Warks CV12 0LY
Tel: 01203 365049

Ford Cortina Mk III Owners
**   Register**
SAE to Keith Macey
Bron Eryri
Nebo
Caernarfon
Gwynedd LL54 6EN
Tel: 01286 881424 (evenings)

Ford Cortina 1600E Owners
**   Club, including 1600E**
**   Savage Register**
SAE to Mr D. Johnson
23 Celandine Avenue
Locksheath
Southampton SO3 6WY

Ford Cortina Owners Club
37 New Road
Weston Turnville
Bucks HP22 5RA
Tel: 01269 613198

The Savage Register
For all Jeff Uren (race-proved)
*   converted Fords*
SAE to Gary Snelling
19 Millway Road
Andover
Hants SP10 3EU
Tel:/Fax: 01264 352774

Ford Avo Owners Club
For Escort Twin-cam, RS1600,
*   Mexico MkI RS2000 and Capri*
*   RS3100*
SAE to Gareth Richards
54 Banners Gate Road
Bridgewood
Sutton Coldfield
West Midlands B73 6RU

Ford Escort Mk I Owners and
**   Enthusiast Club, incorpo-**
**   rating Mk I Register**
SAE to L. Cross
1 Port Lane
Colchester CO1 2JF

Ford Escort 1300E Owners Club
SAE to Steven Ramek
93 Thorkhill Road
Thames Ditton
Surrey KT7 0UQ

Sporting Escort Owners Club
*For non-RS/AVO rear-wheel
    drive Escorts*
SAE to Peter Ridgewell
30 Rowan Way
Thurston
Bury St. Edmunds
Suffolk IP31 3PU

Ford Executive Owners Register
*For Corsair 2000E, Escort 1300E,
    Cortina 1600E/2000E, Capri
    3000E and Zodiac Executive*
SAE to Jenny Whitehouse
3 Shanklin Road
Stonehouse Estate
Coventry

Ford Granada Mk I Owners Club, incorporating the Mk II Register
A5 SAE to Mike Moore
5 Borrowdale Croft
Yeadon
Leeds LS19 7FN
Tel: 01532 509943

Ford Granada Mk II/III Enthusiasts Club
SAE to 515a Bristol Road
Bournbrook
Birmingham B29 6AU
Tel: 0121 426 2346

Ford Granada Mk I and Mk II Drivers Guild
Terry Head
13 Scarsbrook Road
Kidbrooke
London SE3 8AF
Tel: 0181 856 2406

Ford Granada Mk I, II and III Club
Adrian Adams
46 Rowan Drive
Turnford
Herts EN10 6HH
Tel: 01992 440016

Ford Granada Mk II Owners Club
Dave Smith
10 Cross Keys Close
Oak Lane
Sevenoaks
Kent TN13 2TQ
Tel: 01732 462103

The Ford RS Owners Club
SAE to PO Box 717
Seaford
Sussex BN25 4ZR
Tel: 01323 899964

Ford Sidevalve Owners Club
*For small Fords from 1932 Model
Y to 1962 100E/107E*
SAE to 30 Earls Close
Bishopstoke
Eastleigh
Hants SO50 8HY

Ford Model T Ford Register of GB
SAE to Mrs Julie Armer
3 Riverside
Strong Close
Keighley
West Yorkshire
Tel: 01535 607978

Ford Taunus Owners Club of Great Britain
Helaena Massey
Tel: 01384 392192

Ford VS Club
For 1932-53 flat-head Fords
SAE to Stuart Wade
5 Woodlands
Coxheath
Maidstone
Kent ME17 4EE
Tel: 01622 741606

The Ford Y and C Model Register
For Y 1932-37 and C 1934-37
SAE to Bob Wilkinson
Castle Farm
Main Street
Pollington
Near Goole
Humberside
Tel:/Fax: 01405 860836

XR Owners Club
Large SAE to PO Box 47
Loughborough
Leics LE11 1XS

The Frisky Register
John Meadows
Graces Cottage
Tregagle
Monmouth
Gwent NP5 4RZ
Tel: 01600 860420

The Gentry Register
*For owners and constructors of
    RMB Gentry*
SAE to Frank Tuck
1 Kinross Avenue
South Ascot
Berks SL5 9EP
Tel: 01344 24637

Gilbern Owners Club
SAE to B.G. Fawkes
PO Box 43
Letchworth
Herts SG6 4NS

Ginetta Owners Club
For all models from G2 to G33
Roger Bryson
1 Furse Avenue
St. Albans
Herts AL4 9NQ
Tel: 01727 842776

Gordon Keeble Owners Club
Ann Knott
Westminster Road
Brackley
Northants NN13 5EB
Tel: 01280 702311/Fax: 01280
    702853

**The Association of Healey
    Owners**
*For Warwick-built Healeys pre-
    1955*
John Wadsworth
Apartment 4
Stackhouses
Bank Parade
Burnley
Lancs BB1 2TS
Tel: 01282 413458

**Heinkel Trojan Owners and
    Enthusiasts Club**
Large SAE to Peter Jones
37 Brinklow Close
Matchborough West
Redditch
Worcs B98 0HB

Hillman Owners Club
Miss M. Joy
Louise House
Newton
Henlow
Beds SG16 6AJ

**Avenger Sunbeam Owners
    Club**
SAE to 75 Church Drive
South Kirby
Pontefract
West Yorkshire

Historic Rally Car Register
Alison Woolley
Tibberton Court
Tibberton
Glos GL19 3AF
Tel: 01452 790648/Fax: 01452
790703

Historic Sports Car Club
Swindon Road
Kington Langley
Wiltshire SN15 5LY
Fax: 01249 758188

The Holden UK Register
SAE to G.R.C. Hardy
Clun Felin
Wolf's Castle
Haverfordwest
Pembrokeshire
Dyfed SA62 5LR

Honda S600 Sports Car Club
23a High Street
Steeton
West Yorkshire
BD20 6NT
Tel: 01535 653845

Humber Register
For motorcycles/cars to 1932
SAE to R. Arman
175 York Road
Broadstone
Dorset BH18 8ES
Tel: 01202 695937

**Post-Vintage Humber Car
  Club**
For Humbers 1931-76
SAE to N. Gibbins
32 Walsh Crescent
New Addington
Croydon
Surrey CR0 0BX
Tel: 01689 849851

The Imp Club
For Hillman Imp variants
SAE to 31 Abbey Road
Far Cotton
Northampton NN4 8EY

Isotta Owners Club
*For Isotta, BMW 600 and 700
  models*
SAE to Alan Tozer
The Spinney
Fairmile
Henley-on-Thames
Oxon RG9 6AE

Jaguar Club Car
Jeff Holman
Barbary
Chobham Road
Horsell
Woking
Surrey GU21 4AS

Jaguar Drivers Club Ltd
Jaguar House
18 Stuart Street
Luton LU12SL
Tel: 01582 419332

Jaguar Enthusiasts Club
Freepost
Patchway
Bristol BS12 6BR
Tel: 01272 698186

Jaguar and Daimler Owners Club
Mainly XJ6/12, XJS and Sovereigns
Wally Crooks
116 Sherwood Road
Hall Green
Birmingham

Jensen Owners Club
Brian Morrey
Selwood
Howley
Chard
Somerset TA20 3DX
Tel: 01460 64165

The Jensen Club
45 Station Road
Stoke Mandeville
Bucks HP22 5UE
Tel: 01296 614072

Jowett Car Club
Ian Aitken-Kemp
Greenview
High Street
Earlston
Berwickshire TD4 6HQ
Tel: 0189 684 8031

Jupiter Owners Auto Club
David Taylor
319 Markfield Lane
Markfield
Leics LE67 9PR

The Lagonda Club
SAE to Mr J.C. Bulger
Wintney House
London Road
Hartley Wintney
Hants RG27 8RN

Rapier Register
All Lagonda Rapier and Rapier cars
SAE to Mr D.C.H. Williams
The Smithy
Tregynon
Newtown
Powys SY16 3EH
Tel: 01686 650396

Lada Owners Club of GB
Heather Rogers
10 Carnaby Close
Godmanchester
Huntingdon
Cambs PE18 8EE
Tel: 01480 391343

Lancia Motor Club
David Baker
Mount Pleasant
Penhros
Brymbo
Wrexham
Clwyd LL11 5LY

Land Rover 1947-51 Register
*For Early Series 1 80in Land-
    Rovers*
Richard Lines
Ricoli
Conisholme Road
North Somercotes
Louth
Lincs LN11 7PS
Tel:/fax: 01507 358314

Land Rover Series One Club
For vehicles up to 1958
SAE to David Bowyer
East Foldhay
Zeal Monachorum
Crediton
Devon
Tel: 01363 82666

Land Rover Series Two Club
*For all Land Rovers 1958-71,
    including 2A and 2B Forward
    Control*
SAE to PO Box 1750
Bridport
Dorset DT6 5YJ

Lea Frances Owners Club
R. Sawers
French's
Long Wittenham
Abingdon OX14 4QQ
Tel: 01865 407515

Lincoln-Zephyr Owners Club
*For Lincoln-Zephyrs (1936-48)
    and Lincolns*
SAE to Colin Spong
22 North Road
Hainault
Ilford
IG6 2XG

Lotus Cortina Register
*For Mk I and Mk II Lotus
    Cortinas*
SAE to Nethermore Farm
Naish Hill
Lacock
Near Chippenham
Wilts SN15 2QM

Lotus Drivers Club
Peter Cowling
9 Boyleston Road
Hall Green
Birmingham B28 9JN

Lotus Seven Owners Club
For all Lotus/Caterham Sevens
BM Box 8248
London WC1N 3XX
Tel/fax: 01483 277172

Club Lotus
PO Box 8
Dereham
Norfolk NR19 1TF
Tel: 01362 694459

Historic Lotus Register
*For pre-1960 Lotus Sports and
    competition cars*
Victor Thomas
Badgers Farm
Short Green
Winfarthing
Norfolk IP22 2EE
Tel: 01953 860508

Marcos Owners Club
SAE to 51 London Lane
Bromley
Kent
BR1 4HB
Tel: 0181 460 3511

Club Marcos International
SAE to The Spinney
Littleworth Lane
Whitley
Melksham
Wilts SN12 8RE

**Marendaz Special Car
    Register**
John Shaw
107 Old Bath Road
Cheltenham GL53 7DA
Tel: 01242 526310

Maserati Club
Michael Miles
The Paddock
Abbotts Ann
Andover
Hants SP11 7NT

Matra Enthusiasts Club
*For all Matras, including M530,
    Rancho and Renault Espace*
SAE to Greg Dalgleish
The Hollies
Crowborough Hill
Crowborough
East Sussex TN6 2HH
Tel: 01892 652964

Mazda RX-7 Owners Club
SAE to Des Sullivan
44 Tower Close
Charlton
Near Andover
Hants SP10 4RS
Tel: 01264 353625

Mercedes-Benz Club
SAE to Brighstone
Over Old Road
Hartpury
Glos GL19 3BJ
Tel: 01204 309219

The Messerschmitt Owners Club
SAE to E. Hallam
The Birches
Ashmores Lane
Rusper
West Sussex RH12 4PS

The Messerschmitt Enthusiasts Club
SAE to Graham Taylor
5 The Green
Highworth
Swindon
Wiltshire
Tel: 01793 764770

The MG Car Club
13 registers, including all models from 1923 to date
SAE to Kimber House
PO Box 251
Abingdon
Oxon OX14 1FF
Tel: 01235 555552/Fax: 01235 533755

MG Octagon Car Club
For pre-'56 MGs
SAE to Harry Crutchley
36 Queensville Avenue
Stafford ST17 4LS
Tel: 01785 51014

MG Owners Club
SAE to Freepost
Swavesey
Cambridge CR4 1BR
Tel: 01954 31125

The MG Y Type Register
SAE to Mr J.G. Lawson
12 Nithsdale Road
Liverpool L15 5AX

Midget and Sprite Club
For Frog-eyes to 1500s
SAE to Nigel Williams
7 Kings Avenue
Hanham
Bristol BS15 3JN

British Mini Owners Club
Martin Boden
93 Tansey Green Road
Pensnett
Brierley Hill
West Midlands DY5 4TL
Tel: 01384 75296

Mini Cooper Club
SAE to Mary Fowler
38 Arbour House
Arbour Square
London E1 0PP
Tel: 0171 790 7060

Mini Cooper Register
SAE to Alison Clark
6 Willows Road
Bourne End
Bucks SL8 5HG

Mini Owners Club
SAE to 15 Birchwood Road
Lichfield WS14 9UN

Club Mini Classics
*Mainly pre-1969 Minis, other
   Minis, Wolseley Hornets, Riley
   Elfs and Mokes*
Phil Buttifant
54 Wenlock Lane
Great Sutton
South Wirral

Mini Macros Owners Club
*Also for Mini Jem and Kingfisher
   Sprint*
SAE to Roger Garland
28 Meadow Road
Claines
Worcester WR3 7PP
Tel: 01905 458533

Mini Moke Club
SAE to Ian Hodgson
Highgate
Leys Lane
Meriden CV7 7LQ

Mini Seven Racing Club
Mr M. Jackson
345 Clay Lane
South Yardley
Birmingham B26 1ES

Morgan Sports Car Club
For four-wheeled Morgan fans
SAE to Mrs C.L. Healey
41 Cordwell
Castle Donington
Derby DE7 2JL

Bullnose Morris Club
*For all Morris cars and commer-
   cials 1913-1930*
SAE to Richard Harris
PO Box 3838
East Sussex BN3 4FX

Morris Cowley and Oxford Club

For Oxfords/Cowleys/Isis 1954-60
SAE to Derek Andrews
202 Chantry Gardens
Southwick
Trowbridge
Wilts BA14 9QX
Tel: 01225 766800

Morris Marina Owners Club

For Marinas and Itals
SAE to PO Box 84
Stourbridge
West Midlands DY8 1LW

Morris Minor Owners Club

For all 1948-71 Morris Minors
SAE to Jane White
127-129 Green Lane
Derby DE1 1RZ

Morris Minor Owners Club (Northern Ireland)

Miss Joanne Fallis
52 Clonduff Drive
Belfast BT6 9NS
Tel: 01232 791693

Morris Register

For vehicles built before 1940
SAE to Arthur Peeling
171 Levita House
Chalton Street
London NW1 1HR

Morris J Type Register

Also Austin 101s
SAE to 31 Queens Wood Road
Moseley
Birmingham B13 9AU

Moss Owners Club, incorporating Midge and Locust Register

SAE to Steve Jarbutt
89 London Road South
Merstham
Surrey RH1 3AX
Tel: 01737 645165

Friends of the National Motor Museum

Mr M. Ware
Beaulieu
Brockenhurst
Hants SO42 7ZN
Tel: 01590 612345

Mustang Owners Club of GB

SAE to April Keighley
21 Raleigh Close
Eaton Socon
St. Neots
Huntingdon
Cambs PE19 3NN
Tel: 01480 477254

NSU Owners Club
Rosemarie Crowley
58 Tadorne Road
Tadworth
Surrey KT20 5TF
Tel: 01737 812412

Ro80 Club GB
Eric Dalton
9 Manor Close
Congleton
Cheshire CW12 3LB
Tel: 01260 272707

The Ogle Register
Chris Gow
108 Potters Lane
Burgess Hill RH15 9JN
Tel: 01444 248439

The Autobahn Stormers
For Monzas, Royales & Senators
Charley Brighton
34 Juniper Way Hayes
Middx UB3 1LE
Tel: 0181 813 6664

Opel GT UK Owners Club
SAE to Dean Hayes
11 Thrale Way
Rainham
Gillingham
Kent ME8 9LX
Tel: 01634 379065

The Opel Manta Club
For all Mantas Series A to 400
SAE to 14 Rockstowes Way
Westbury-on Trym
Bristol BS10 6JE

Panther Car Club Ltd
George Newell
91 Fleet Road
Farnborough
Hants GU14 9RE
Tel: 01252 540217

Club Peugeot UK
SAE to Dick Kitchingman
Pelham
Chideock
Bridport DT6 6JW

The Piper (Sports and Racing Car) Club
For road-going GTT and P2 types, GTR and other racing models
Clive Davies
Pipers Oak
Lopham Road
East Harling
Norfolk
Tel: 01953 717813

Porsche Club Great Britain
Ayton House
West End
Northleach
Glos GL54 3HG
Tel: 01451 860792

**The Post-War Thoroughbred
  Car Club**
SAE to 87 London Street
Chertsey
Surrey KT16 8AN

The Radford Register
*For all Harold Radford-
  converted cars*
Chris Gow
108 Potters Lane
Burgess Hill
West Sussex
Tel: 01444 248439

Railton Owners Club
*For Railtons, Brough Superiors
  and all Hudsons*
SAE to Fairmiles
Barnes Hall Road
Sheffield S30 4RF
Tel: 01742 468357

**Raleigh Safety Seven and
  Early Reliant Owners Club**
*For Raleigh motorcycles, three-
  wheelers and pre-1962 Reliants*
SAE Mick Sleap
17 Courtland Avenue
London E4 6DU

Range Rover Register
SAE to Victor Jones
139 Woodbrook Road
Abbey Wood
London SE2 0PB

Reliant Owners Club
SAE to Graham Chappell
19 Smithey Close
High Green
Sheffield S30 4FQ

Reliant Rebel Register
*For four-wheeler saloons, vans
  and estates*
SAE to Terry Scott
36 Cannon Way
Fetcham
Surrey KT2 29IJ

**Scimitar Drivers Club
  International**
SAE to Liam Hayden
1 Ashvale Gardens
Cranham
Upminster
Essex
Tel: 01708 225807

Reliant Sabre and Scimitar Owners Club
For all Reliant sports cars
SAE to PO Box 67
Teddington TW11 8QR
Tel: 0181 977 6625

Club Alpine-Renault (GB) Ltd
Peter Whitehouse
1 Bloomfield Close
Wombourne
Wolverhampton WV5 8HQ
Tel: 01902 895590

Rear Engine Renault Club
SAE to Kevin Gould
2 Barley Field Close
Heighington
Lincoln LN4 1TX

Renault Owners Club
For all post-war Renaults
SAE to 12 Freeby Avenue
Mansfield Woodhouse
Mansfield
Notts NG19 9HS

Riley Motor Club Ltd
SAE to J.S. Hall
Treelands
127 Penn Road
Wolverhampton WV3 0DU

The Riley Register
For Rileys 1899-1940
SAE to J.A. Clark
56 Cheltenham Road
Bishops Cleeve
Cheltenham
Glos GL52 4LY
Tel: 01242 673598

Riley RM Club
Jacque Manders
Y Fachell
Ruthin Road
Gwernymynydd
Near Mold
Clywd CH7 5LQ
Tel: 01352 700427

Rochdale Owners Club
Alaric Spendlove
7 Whitleigh Avenue
Crownhill
Plymouth PL5 3BQ
Tel: 01752 791409

Rolls-Royce Enthusiasts
*For Rolls-Royces and Bentleys
from 1904 to date*
Lt. Col. E. Barrass
The Hunt House
Paulersbury
Northants NN12 7NA

Rover P4 Drivers Guild
SAE to Colin Blowers
32 Arundel Road
Luton
Beds LU4 8DY
Tel: 01582 572499

Rover P5 Owners Club
SAE to G. Moorshead
13 Glen Avenue
Ashford
Middx TW15 2JE
Tel: 01784 258166

P6 Rover Owners Club
SAE to PO Box 11
Heanor
Derbyshire DE7 7YG
Fax: 01773 535250

Rover P6 Drivers Club
SAE to 103 Hollyhock Road
Acocks Green
Birmingham B27 7SY

Rover SD1 Club
SAE to PO Box 12
Owlsmoor
Camberley GU15 4WZ
Tel: 01344 761791

Rover Sports Register
SAE to C.S. Evans
8 Hilary Close
Great Boughton
Chester CH3 5QP

Saab Enthusiasts
For all pre-1980 Saabs
Tom Noonan
29 Claremont
Bricket Wood
St. Albans
Tel: 01923 672388

The Saab Owners Club of GB
Mrs K.E. Piper
16 Denewood Close
Watford
Herts WD1 3SZ
Tel: 01923 229945

British Salmson Owners Club
John Maddison
86 Broadway North
Walsall
West Midlands
WS1 2QF
Tel: 01922 29677

Salmons Tickford Enthusiasts Club
For all coachwork or conversions up to and including 1959
Neville Clarke
5 The Elms Paddock
Clifton upon Dunsmore
Rugby CV23 0TD
Tel: 01788 537695

Simca Owners Register
For all Simcas and related Talbots
David Chapman
18 Cavendish Gardens
Redhill
Surrey RH1 4AQ

Singer Owners Club
Martyn Wray
11 Ermine Rise
Great Casterton
Stamford
Lincs PE9 4AJ
Tel: 01780 62740

Association of Singer Car Owners
Anne Page
39 Oakfield
Rickmansworth
Herts WD3 2LR
Tel: 01923 778575

Skoda Owners Club of GB
SAE to 10 Woburn House
Woburn Avenue
Theydon Bois
Epping CM16 7LH

Spartan Owners Club
SAE to Steven Andrews
28 Ashford Drive
Ravenhead
Notts
Tel: 01623 793742

Atlas Register
For standard Atlases and derivatives, including Leyland 15 and 20
SAE to 38 Ridgeway
Southwell
Notts NG25 0DU

Standard Vanguard Owners Club
For Phase I and Phase II models
Ken Holstead
7 Priory Close
Wilton
Salisbury
Wilts SP2 0LD

Vanguard 3 Owners Club
SAE to Martin Holstead
14 Kennet Rise
Axford
Marlborough
Wilts SN8 2EZ
Tel: 01672 20154

Standard Motor Club
*For Vanguards, Ensigns, 8 and
   10s, Flyers and all pre-war
   models*
Tony Pingriff
57 Main Road
Meriden
Coventry CV7 7LP
Tel: 01676 522181

**Star, Starling, Stuart and
   Briton Register**
*For vehicles made by Star and
   Briton companies*
D.E.A. Evans
New Wood Lodge
2A Hyperion Road
Stourton
Stourbridge DY7 6SB

**Sunbeam Rapier Owners
   Club**
SAE to Peter Meech
12 Greenacres
Downton
Salisbury
Wilts SP5 3NG
Tel: 01725 511140

**Sunbeam Alpine Owners
   Club**
*For Rootes Group Alpines and
   Harringtons 1959-68*
SAE to PO Box 93
Reigate
Surrey RH2 7TF

**Sunbeam Talbot Alpine
   Owners Club**
SAE to Faye Barringer-Capp
3 Lammermoor Road
Mossley Hill
Liverpool L18 4QP
Tel: 0151 724 4063

**Sunbeam Talbot Darracq
   Register**
*For pre-1935 Sunbeams and
   Talbots, Roesch Talbots,
   Darracqs and Lago Talbots*
SAE to B. Donovan
Clackwell House
Stubbs Wood
Chesham Bois
Amersham HP6 6EY

Sunbeam Tiger Owners Club
For Tiger 260/289s
SAE to Brian Postle
Beechwood
8 Villa Real Estate
Consett
Co. Durham DH8 6BJ

Swift Club and Swift Register
John Harrison
70 Eastwick Drive
Great Bookham
Leatherhead
Surrey KT23 3NX
Tel: 01372 452120

Trident Car Club
Ken Morgan
Rose Cottage
Black Hill
Verwood
Dorset BH31 6HA
Tel: 01202 822697

Tornado Register
*Also for Typhoon, Tempest and
    Talisman*
SAE to Dave Malins
48 St Monica's Avenue
Luton
Beds LU3 1PN
Tel: 01582 37641

Toyota Enthusiasts Club
SAE to Billy Wells
28 Park Road
Feltham
Middlesex TW13 6PW
Tel: 0181 898 0740

Toyota MR2 Drivers Club
Ken Kinnersley
555 Lincoln Road
Peterborough
PE1 2PB
Tel: 01733 327474

**Triumph Sporting Owners
    Club**
SAE to P. Utratny
57 Rothiemey Road
Flixton
Urmston
Manchester M31 3JY

Club Triumph Eastern
SAE to Peter Condon
193 Mawney Road
Romford
Essex RM7 8BX
Tel: 01708 705365

Club Triumph
Derek Pollock
Freepost
86 Waggon Road
Hadley Wood
Herts EN4 0PP
Tel: 0181 440 9000/Fax: 0181
    440 4694

**Pre-1940 Triumph Owners
    Club**
From Triumph cars 1923-40
Ian Harper
155 Winkworth Road
Banstead
Surrey SM7 2JP

Triumph Dolomite Club
*For Dolomite 1300/1500 fwd
    Toledo and Dolomite-derived
    kit cars*
39 Mill Lane
Arncott
Bicester
Oxon OX6 0PB
Tel: 01869 242847

Triumph Mayflower Club
SAE to John Oaker
19 Broadway North
Walsall
West Midlands WS1 2QG
Tel: 01922 33042

**Triumph Razoredge Owners
    Club**
*For 1800, 2000 and Renowns
    1946-55*
SAE to Stewart Langton
62 Seaward Avenue
Barton-on-Sea
Hants
Tel: 01425 618074

The Triumph Roadster Club
*For 1946-49 1800cc and 2000cc
    Roadsters*
Mr A. Hill
17 Nursery Grove
Ecclesfield
Sheffield
South Yorkshire S30 3XW

Triumph Spitfire Club
SAE to Cor Gent
Anemoon 41
7483 AC
Haaksbergen
The Netherlands

Triumph Sports Six Club Ltd
*For Herald, Spitfire, Vitesse, GT6,
    Bond Equipe and Specials*
Freepost
Lubenham
Market Harborough
Leics LE16 9TF
Tel: 01858 434424/Fax: 01858
    431936

Stag Owners Club
SAE to Howard Vesey
53 Cyprus Road
Faversham
Kent ME13 8HD

TR Drivers Club
SAE to 40 Carr Lane
Hawkley Hall
Wigan
WN3 5ND
Tel: 01942 498001

The TR Register
*For TR2 to TR8, and 1B
    Hawksworth*
Southmead Industrial Park
Didcot
Oxon OX11 7HR
Tel: 01235 818866

**Triumph 2000/2500/2.5
    Register**
Mirium Aldous
42 Hall Orchards
Middleton
Kings Lynn PE32 1RY
Tel: 01553 841700

**Triumph 2000, 2500 Owners
    Club**
Miss B. Dowsing
18 Meadowcroft Close
Glenfield
Leicester LE3 8QX
Tel: 01533 314414

TVR Car Club
SAE to 21 Hawkswood Road
Woodlands
Cheltenham GL15 5DT

Vanden Plas Owners Club
*For Vanden Plas-bodied cars from
    1923*
SAE to Nigel Stephens
The Briars
Lawson Leas
Barrowby
Grantham
Lincs

Vauxhall Owners Club
For all 1903-57 E Series
SAE to Brian Mundell
2 Flaxron Court
St. Leonard's Road
Ayr KA7 2PP

Vauxhall-Opel Drivers Club
32a High Street
Dereham
Norfolk NR19 1DR
Tel: 01362 691144/694459

Droop Snoot Group
For Firenzas, Sports Hatches, HS Chevettes, Viva and Magnum
SAE to 28 Second Avenue
Ravenswing Park
Aldermaston
Reading
Berks
Tel: 01734 815238

Royal Monza Owners Club International
For Vauxhall Royale coupé and Opel Monza
SAE to Diane Dempsey
8 Monks Hill
Saffron Walden
Essex CB11 3BW
Tel: 01799 523748

Vauxhall PA/PB/PC/E Owners Club
SAE to Steve Chapman
333 Eastcote Lane
South Harrow
Middx HA2 8RY

Vauxhall Victor Owners Club
For 1957-67 models
SAE to Dept 2
27 Northville Drive
Westcliff-on-Sea
Essex SS0 0QA
Tel: 01702 345885

Victor 101 Club
For all Bedford CAs/CFs and Vauxhall F/FB/FC/PA/PB/PCs
SAE to Mrs J. Caldwell
43 Princess Street
Widnes WA8 6NT

The Viva Owners Club
For HA, HB and HC Vivas
SAE to Adrian Miller
The Thatches
Snetterton North End
Snetterton
Norwich NR16 2LD
Tel: 01953 498818

Vauxhall VX4/90 Club
For all FD, FE and VX Victors, Ventoras and VX4/90s for 1968-78
Large SAE to 26 Keresley Road
Keresley
Coventry CV6 2JD

Veteran Car Club of Great Britain
For pre-1919 cars
SAE to Jessamine Court
15 High Street
Ashwell
Herts SG7 5NL
Tel: 0462 742818

Vintage Sports Car Club Ltd
*For pre-1931 cars and selected
  makes up to 1940*
121 Russell Road
Newbury
Berks RG14 5JX
Tel: 01635 44411/Fax: 01635
  580612

**The Association of British
  Volkswagen Clubs**
66 Pinewood Green
Iver Heath
Bucks

**Volkswagen Owners Club
  (GB)**
SAE to PO Box 7
Burntwood
Walsall
Staffs WS7 8SB

Historic Volkswagen Club
SAE to Rod Sleigh
28 Longnor Road
Brooklands
Telford
Shropshire TF1 3NY
Tel: 01952 242167

Volvo Enthusiasts Club
For pre-1979 cars
SAE to Kevin Price
4 Goonbell
St. Agnes
Cornwall TR5 0PH
Tel: 01872 553740

Volvo Owners Club
SAE to John Smith
18 Macaulay Avenue
Portsmouth
Hants PO6 4NY
Tel:/fax: 01705 381494

**The Wartburg IFA Owners
  Club**
Also for other DDR vehicles
John Everson
43 Robertson Street
Battersea
London SW8 3TX

**Wolseley 6/80 and Morris MO
  Oxford Club**
SAE to Don Gould
2 Barleyfield Close
Heighington
Lincs LN4 1TX

The Wolseley Hornet Special Club
For 1930-36 cars
Sandy Ellin
The Poppies
9 Cole Mead
Bruton
Somerset BA10 0DL

Wolseley Register
SAE to Mr A. Murray
Corylus
Bolton Percy
York YO5 7AD

Selective List of UK Motor Museums

ENGLAND

London

Imperial War Museum
D.J. Penn (Keeper)
Lambeth Road SE1 6HZ

London Transport Museum
M. Dennison (Curator)
Covent Garden WC2E 7BB

Science Museum
P. Mann (Curator)
Exhibition Road SW7 2DD

Avon

Bristol Industrial Museum
P.W. Elkin (Curator)
Prince's Wharf
Prince Street
Bristol BS1 4RN

**Weston-super-Mare Motoring
and Memorabilia Museum**
C.H. Jacobs (Curator)
Chestnut House
4 Chestnut Chase
Nailsea BS19 1QB

Bedfordshire

**Fire Services National
Museum**
M. Cole (Curator)
9 Morland Way
Manton Heights
Bedford MK41 7NP

Shuttleworth Collection
P. Symes (Manager)
Old Warden Aerodrome
Biggleswade SG18 9ER

**Stondon Museum and Garden
Centre**
Station Road
Lower Stondon
Henlow SG16 6JN

Vauxhall Heritage Centre
B. Ridgeley (Curator)
Griffin House
PO Box 3
Osborne Road
Luton LU2 0SY

Berkshire

Museum of English Rural Life
R. Brigden (Curator)
The University
Whiteknights Park
Reading

Royal Electrical and Mechanical Engineers Museum
Lt. Col. (retd) M.W. LeVar (Curator)
Isaac Newton Road
Arborfield Garrison
Arborfield
Reading RG2 9LN

Buckinghamshire

Dewsbury Bus Museum
D. Crowther (Administrator)
1a Barberswood Close
Booker
High Wycombe HP12 4EW

West Wycombe Motor Museum
Mrs S. Wood (Curator)
Cockshoot Farm
Chorley Wood
West Wycombe

Cambridgeshire

Duxford Airfield Imperial War Museum
D.M. Fearon (Vehicle Officer)
Duxford
Cambridge CB2 4QR

Cheshire

Mouldsworth Motor Museum
J. Peacop (Curator)
The Balcony House
Erindale Crescent
Frodsham WA6 6DZ

Cornwall

Automobilia
C. Vincent (Curator)
The Old Mill
St. Stephen
St. Austell

Museum of Historic Cycling
S. and J. Middleton (Curators)
The Old Station
Camelford PL32 9TZ

Cumbria

Cars of the Stars Museum
P. Nelson (Curator)
c/o Fitz Park House
Keswick CA12 5HH

Lakeland Motor Museum
E.L. Maher (Commercial
    Manager)
Holker Hall
Cark in Cartmel LA11 7PL

Levens Hall Steam Collection
C.H. Bagot (Curator)
Levens Hall
Kendal LA8 0PD

Westmorland Motor Museum
C. Booth (Curator)
Rellandsgate
Kings Meaburn
Penrith CA10 3BT

Derbyshire

Donington Collection
A. Melson (Curator)
Donington Park
Castle Donington DE7 2RP

Devon

Cobbaton Combat Collection
P. Isaac (Curator)
Chittlehampton
Umberleigh

**Combe Martin Motorcycle
    Collection**
T.C. McCulley (Curator)
Cross Street
Combe Martin EX34 0DH

Lambretta Museum
Mrs R. Karslake (Curator)
Kesterfield
Northlew
Okehampton EX20 3PN

Motoring Memories
R. Barnard (Curator)
Darracott
Gravel Lane
Seaton

National Ambulance Museum
T. Paddon-Hall (Director)
Harford Bridge
Peter Tavy
Tavistock PO19 9LR

Totnes Motor Museum
R. Pilkington (Curator)
Steamer Quay
Totnes TQ9 5AL

**West of England Transport
    Collection**
C. Shears (Curator)
9 Hillcrest Park
Pennsylvania
Exeter EX4 4SH

Dorset

Bournemouth Transport Museum
Mr Jeffrey (Managing Director)
Building 101
Northwest Industrial Estate
Bournemouth (Hurn)
International Airport
Hurn
Christchurch BH23 6NW

Christchurch Tricycle Museum
R. Street (Curator)
Quay Road
Christchurch BH23 1BY

The Motor House
Ms S. Heavens (Curator)
Christchurch Ski and Leisure
Centre
Matchams Lane
Hurn
Christchurch BH23 6AW

Tank Museum
J. Woodward (Curator)
Bovington Camp
Wareham BH20 6JG

Durham

North of England Open-Air Museum
J. Gall (Curator)
Beamish DH9 0RG

East Sussex

Bentley Wildfowl and Motor Museum
H. Stuart-Roberts (Curator)
Halland
Lewes BN8 5AF

Filching Manor Motor Museum
P. Foulkes-Halbard (Curator)
Filching Manor
Wannock
Polegate TN26 5QA

Essex

Battlesbridge Motorcycle Museum
D. Evans (Curator)
Battlesbridge Antiques Centre
1 Maltings Road
Battlesbridge SS11 7RF

Castle Point Transport Museum
5 Barncombe Close
Thundersley
Benfleet SS7 4AQ

Gloucestershire

Cotswold Motor Museum
M.N. Cavanagh (Curator)
The Old Mill
Bourton on the Water

Greater Manchester

Manchester Museum of Transport
D. Talbot (Chairman)
Boyle Street
Cheetham Hill M8 8UL

Hampshire

Braemore Countryside Museum
J.E. Forshaw (Curator)
Fordingbridge SP6 2DF

National Motor Museum
Michael Ware (Curator)
Beaulieu
Brockenhurst SO42 7ZN

Sammy Miller Motorcycle Museum
S. Miller (Curator)
Gore Road
New Milton

Hertfordshire

MG Museum
39 Baldock Road
Letchworth SG6 3JX

Humberside

Hull Transport Museum 'Streetlife'
S. Goodhand (Keeper)
36 High Street
Kingston upon Hull

Museum of Army Transport
W.A. Dugan (Technical Curator)
Beverley HU17 0NG

Kent

Canterbury Motor Museum
C. May (Curator)
11 Cogans Terrace
Canterbury CT1 3SJ

Dover Transport Museum
C. Smith (Curator)
33 Alfred Road
Dover CT16 2AD

**Historic Vehicles Collection
of C.M. Booth**
C.M. Booth (Curator)
63-67 High Street
Rolvenden
Cranbrook TN17 4LP

Ramsgate Motor Museum
T. Sharpe (Curator)
Westcliff Hall
Ramsgate CT11 9JX

Lancashire

**British Commercial Vehicle
Museum**
P. Dawson (Manager)
King Street
Leyland
Preston PR5 1LE

**National Museum of Police
Motor Vehicles**
J. Dillon (Acting General
Manager)
Yealand Conyers
Carnforth

**Tameside Transport
Collection**
Mr Howarth (Curator)
Warlow Brook
Frietland
Greenfield
Oldham

Leicestershire

**Stanford Hall Motorcycle
Museum**
C.E. Allen (Curator)
Lutterworth LE17 6DH

Lincolnshire

**Geeson Brothers Motorcycle
Museum and Workshop**
G. Geeson (Curator)
South Witham
Grantham NG33 5PH

**Lincolnshire Road Transport
Museum**
S. Milner (Curator)
3 The Paddock
High Street
Skellingthorpe LN6 5TR

National Cycle Museum
Mrs S.E. Beeley (Curator)
Brayford Wharf North
Lincoln LN1 1YW

UK MOTOR MUSEUMS

Merseyside

St. Helens Transport Museum
T. Lynas (Director)
Old Bus Depot
Hall Street
St. Helens WA10 1DU

Norfolk

Bressingham Steam Museum
A. Bloom (Director)
Bressingham
Diss IP22 2AB

Caister Castle Motor Museum
P.R. Hill (Curator)
Caister on Sea
Great Yarmouth

Sandringham Museum
Mrs G.M. Pattison (Curator)
Sandringham PE35 6EN

Sandtoft Transport Museum
D. Brown (Curator)
71 Bishops Close
River Green Park
Thorpe St. Andrew
Norwich NR7 0EH

Nottinghamshire

Nottingham Industrial Museum
J. Cox (Secretary)
Courtyard Buildings
Wallaton Park
Nottingham NG8 2AE

Oxfordshire

Oxford Bus Museum
Old Station Yard
Long Hanborough

Shropshire

Haynes Motor Museum
M. Penn (Curator)
Sparkford
Yeovil BA22 7LH

Midland Motor Museum
M. Barker (Curator)
Stanmore Hall
Stourbridge Road
Bridgnorth WV15 6DT

South Yorkshire

Sheffield Bus Museum
D. Roberts (Chairman)
17 Gaunt Drive
Sheffield

Staffordshire

**Potteries Omnibus
  Preservation Society**
N. Brundritt (Curator)
PMT Ltd
33 Woodhouse Street
Stoke on Trent ST4 1EQ

Suffolk

**East Anglia Transport
  Museum**
Mrs A.C. Carr (Curator)
Chapel Road
Carlton Colville
Lowestoft NR33 8BL

Easton Farm Park
C. Barbour (Manager)
Easton
Woodbridge IP13 0EQ

Ipswich Transport Museum
33 Everton Crescent
Ipswich IP1 6DB

Surrey

Brooklands Museum
Mrs M. Barton (Director)
The Clubhouse
Brooklands Road
Weybridge KT13 0QN

Cobham Bus Museum
A. Peters (Curator)
Redhill Road
Cobham KT11 1EF

Kew Transport Museum
M. Wilsden (Curator)
41 Burlington Avenue
Kew Gardens TW9 4DG

The Land Rover Museum
P. Bashall (Curator)
Dunsfold Land Rovers Ltd
Alfold Road
Dunsfold
Godalming GU8 4NP

Tyne and Wear

Military Vehicle Museum
W.G. Tearse (Museum
  Manager)
Exhibition Park Museum
Newcastle upon Tyne NE2 4PZ

**Newburn Hall Motor
  Museum**
T. Porelli (Curator)
35 Townfield Gardens
Newburn NE15 8PY

Northeast Bus Museum
D.G. Slater (Curator)
Leam Lane
Wardley
Gateshead NE10 8YY

Warwickshire

**British Motor Industry
Heritage Trust**
Ms F. Tordoss (Curator)
Heritage Motor Centre
Gaydon CV35 0BJ

**Museum of British Road
Transport**
B.R. Littlewood (Curator)
St. Agnes Lane
Hales Street
Coventry CV1 1PN

West Midlands

**Aston Manor Road Transport
Museum**
W. Staniforth (Secretary)
208-216 Witton Lane
Birmingham B6 6QE

Black Country Museum
I.N. Walden (Director)
Tipton Road
Dudley DY1 4SQ

**Museum of Science and
Industry**
Newhall Street
Birmingham B3 1RZ

National Motorcycle Museum
W.R. Richards (Curator)
Coventry Road
Bickenhill
Solihull B92 0EJ

West Yorkshire

Automobilia
B. Collins (Curator)
Billy Lane
Old Town
Hebden Bridge HX7 8RY

**Bradford Industrial Museum
and Horses at Work**
R. McHugh (Curator)
Moorside Road
Eccleshill
Bradford BD2 3HP

Meltham Mills Bus Museum
Mersey and Calder Bus
Preservation Group
T. Blackman (Curator)
c/o 1 Vicar Park Road
Norton Tower
Halifax HX2 0NL

Yorkshire Car Collection
G. Tuley (Curator)
Grange Street
Keighley BD21 3EJ

Wiltshire

Atwell-Wilson Motor Museum
R. and H. Atwell (Curators)
Downside
Stockley
Calne SN11 0NF

Worcestershire

Birmingham and Midland Motor Omnibus Trust
P. Gray (Curator)
88 Old Station Road
Bromsgrove B60 2AF

ISLE OF MAN

Manx Motor Museum
R. Evans (Curator)
Crosby

Murray's Motorcycle Museum
C. Murray (Curator)
Bungalow Corner (TT Course)
Snaefell Mountain

CHANNEL ISLANDS

Jersey Motor Museum
F.M. Wilcock (Curator)
St. Peter's Village
Jersey JE3 7AG

SCOTLAND

Biggar Museum Trust
B. Lambie (Curator)
Gladstone Court Museum
Biggar ML12 6DT

Doune Motor Museum
J.B. Asher (Curator)
Carse of Cambus
Doune FK16 6HD

Glasgow Museum of Transport
R.A.R. Smith (Curator)
Kelvin Hall
1 Bunhouse Road
Glasgow G3 8DP

Glenluce Motor Museum
B. Adams (Curator)
Glenluce DG8 0NY

Grampian Transport Museum
M. Ward (Curator)
Alford AB33 8AD

Highland Motor Heritage Centre
J.C. Hibbert (Curator)
Bankfoot PH1 4EB

Melrose Motor Museum
W.P. Dale (Curator)
Annay Road
Melrose TD6 9LW

Moray Motor Museum
S. Allen (Curator)
Lossibank Woollen Mills
Bishopmill
Elgin

The Motor Museum
T. Amyes (Curator)
Mill Two
New Lanark Mills
Lanark ML1 9XB

Museum of Fire
Mr McMutrie (Curator)
Lothian and Borders Fire
   Brigade
Lauriston Place
Edinburgh EH3 9DE

Myreton Motorcycle Museum
M. Mutch (Curator)
Aberlady EH32 0PZ

Royal Museum of Scotland
A.G.I. Dodds (Curator)
Chambers Street
Edinburgh EH1 1JF

WALES

Amgueddfa Madog Motor Museum
I. Evans (Curator)
Porthmadog

Betws-y-Coed Motor Museum
A.K. Houghton (Curator)
Betws-y-Coed

Llangollen Motor Museum
A. Broadhurst (Curator)
Pentrefelin
Llangollen

Pembrokeshire Motor Museum
C. Robinson (Managing
   Director)
Keeston Hill
Haverfordwest SA62 6EJ

NORTHERN IRELAND

Ulster Folk and Transport Museum
J. Moore (Curator)
Cultra
Holywood
County Down

COLLINS

Other Collins titles that may interest you include:

Pocket Reference Driving Skills
An invaluable guide for anyone learning to drive, plus highlighted advice from the Highway Code   **£4.99**

Pocket Reference Written Driving Test
An essential guide to this new component of the Driving Text, to be introduced from July 1996   **£4.99**

Collins/Jane's Modern Tanks
A fully illustrated pocket guide to over 250 of today's combat vehicles   **£3.99**

Collins/Jane's Tanks of World War II
A complete guide to over 230 tanks used by all the main armies   **£3.99**

Gem Bike Book
A handy and compact guide to buying, maintaining and safely riding your bike   **£3.50**

COLLINS

Bestselling Collins Gem titles include:

Gem English Dictionary (£3.50)
Gem Calorie Counter (£2.99)
Gem Thesaurus (£2.99)
Gem French Dictionary (£3.50)
Gem German Dictionary (£3.50)
Gem Basic Facts Mathematics (£2.99)
Gem Birds Photoguide (£3.50)
Gem Babies' Names (£2.99)
Gem Card Games (£3.50)
Gem Atlas of the World (£3.50)

All Collins Gems are available from your local bookseller or can be ordered direct from the publishers.

In the UK, contact Mail Order, Dept 2M, HarperCollins Publishers, Westerhill Rd, Bishopbriggs, Glasgow, G64 2QT, listing the titles required and enclosing a cheque or p.o. for the value of the books plus £1.00 for the first title and 25p for each additional title to cover p&p. Access and Visa cardholders can order on 0141-772 2281 (24 hr).

In Australia, contact Customer Services, HarperCollins Distribution, Yarrawa Rd, Moss Vale 2577 (tel. [048] 68 0300). **In New Zealand,** contact Customer Services, HarperCollins Publishers, 31 View Rd, Glenfield, Auckland 10 (tel. [09] 444 3740). **In Canada,** contact your local bookshop.